The Road to Professional Excellence:
A Holistic Guide to Career Success

Laurel D. Malvern

Copyright and Legal Disclaimer

Copyright © 2024 by Laurel D. Malvern. All rights reserved. No part of this book may be reproduced, stored in a retrieval system, or transmitted in any form or by any means — electronic, mechanical, photocopy, recording, or otherwise — without the prior written permission of the publisher, except for brief quotations embodied in critical reviews and certain other noncommercial uses permitted by copyright law.

The information in this book is provided for general informational purposes only. Every effort has been made to ensure that the information is accurate and up-to-date at the time of publication. However, the author and publisher do not warrant or represent that the information is free from errors or omissions. Readers should use their discretion and seek professional advice where necessary, as the content is not intended to substitute personalized guidance or expertise.

The author and publisher shall not be liable for any loss, damage, or injury arising from the use of this book. Your use of this book constitutes your agreement to these terms.

"The Road to Professional Excellence: A Holistic Guide to Career Success"

Preface 7

Chapter 1: The Importance of a Comprehensive Approach to Career Success 10

Chapter 2: Laying the Foundation - Career Advice and Professional Development 11

Chapter 3: Professional Development 13

Chapter 4: Understanding the Fundamentals of Career Planning 24

Chapter 5: Importance of Continuous Learning and Development 39

Chapter 6: Creating a Personalized Professional Development Plan 63

Chapter 7: The Inner Work - Self-Improvement and Building Self-Confidence 67

Chapter 8: Strategies for Personal Growth and Self-Improvement 72

Chapter 9: Developing Self-Confidence in the Workplace 77

Chapter 10: Overcoming Self-Doubt and Impostor Syndrome 82

Chapter 11: The Job Hunt - Navigating the Job Search 87

Chapter 12: Effective Job Search Strategies in a Digital Age 91

Chapter 13: Utilizing Online Platforms and Networking for Job Hunting 95

Chapter 14: Crafting a Compelling Resume and Cover Letter 99

Chapter 15: Defining Your Path - Setting Career Goals 103

Chapter 16: Importance of Setting Clear, Achievable Career Goals 107

Chapter 17: Aligning Personal and Professional Aspirations 111

Chapter 18: Making Your Mark - Personal Branding 115

Chapter 19: Building and Maintaining a Strong Personal Brand 119

Chapter 20: Mastering Communication - Essential Communication Skills 122

Chapter 21: The Role of Effective Communication in Career Success 125

Chapter 22: Techniques and strategies related to active listening and persuasive communication. 129

Chapter 23: "Leading the Way - Developing Leadership Skills," would typically cover the key qualities and attributes that contribute to effective leadership. 131

Chapter 24: "Transitioning from Individual Contributor to Leader: Leadership Styles and When to Use Them," would focus on the challenges and strategies involved in moving from a role focused on individual contributions to one that involves leading and managing others. 134

Chapter 25: Building Connections 137

Chapter 26: Building and Maintaining a Strong Network. 140

Chapter 27: Managing Your Time 143

Chapter 28: Strategies for Effective Time Management" 146

Chapter 29: Prioritizing Tasks and Avoiding Procrastination. 149

Chapter 30: Balancing Workload to Prevent Burnout. 152

Chapter 31: Acing the Interview 155

Chapter 32: Preparing for Different Types of Interviews, Common Interview Questions, and Following Up After the Interview. 158

Chapter 33: Crafting Your Narrative - Effective Resume Writing. 160

Chapter 34: Key Elements of a Standout Resume, Tailoring Your Resume for Specific Roles, and Avoiding Common Resume Mistakes 163

Chapter 35: Embracing Change - Navigating Career Transitions 166

Chapter 36: Identifying When It's Time for a Career Change, Planning and Executing a Successful Career Transition, and Overcoming Challenges During a Career Shift 169

Chapter 37: Balancing Act - Achieving Work-Life Balance 172

Chapter 38: Importance of Work-Life Balance for Long-Term Success, Strategies for Managing Work and Personal Life, Setting Boundaries, and Making Time for Self-Care 175

Chapter 39: Setting the Stage - Goal Setting for Professional Growth 178

Chapter 40: Techniques for Setting and Achieving Professional Goals, Creating Short-Term and Long-Term Career Plans, Evaluating and Adjusting Goals as Needed 181

Chapter 41: Thriving in the Workplace - Understanding Workplace Culture 184

Chapter 42: The Art of Negotiation - Developing Negotiation Skills 187

Chapter 43: Staying Grounded - Stress Management Techniques 190

Chapter 44: The Entrepreneurial Spirit - Exploring Entrepreneurship 193

Chapter 45: Standing Firm - Building Assertiveness in the Workplace 196

Chapter 46: The Growth Mindset - Strategies for Career Growth 199

Chapter 47: Finding Fulfillment - Enhancing Job Satisfaction 202

Conclusion: Your Path Forward 205

Appendix: Resources and Tools 208

Skill Development and Learning Platforms: 211

Comprehensive Index 213

Preface

Dear Reader,

Welcome to "The Road to Professional Excellence: A Holistic Guide to Career Success." Whether you are just starting your career journey, navigating a transition, or seeking to enhance your current professional standing, this book is designed to be your comprehensive companion.

In today's dynamic and competitive world, achieving career success requires more than just technical skills. It demands a holistic approach that encompasses personal growth, effective communication, leadership development, and strategic networking. This book aims to equip you with the tools, strategies, and insights necessary to thrive in any professional environment.

Through my years of experience in mentoring and guiding individuals across various industries, I've witnessed firsthand the transformative power of a well-rounded approach to career development. Each chapter in this book is meticulously crafted to provide practical advice, actionable steps, and thought-provoking insights that you can apply immediately.

From laying the foundation of career planning to mastering the art of negotiation, from enhancing your personal brand to achieving work-life balance, each topic is explored with the intention of empowering you to navigate challenges and seize opportunities effectively.

I encourage you to approach this book not just as a passive reader, but as an active participant in your own professional journey. Take the time to reflect on the exercises, implement the strategies, and adapt the insights to suit your unique aspirations and circumstances.

Remember, career success is not a destination but a continuous journey of growth and learning. As you embark on this road to professional excellence, I hope this book serves as a valuable resource and source of inspiration, guiding you towards realizing your fullest potential.

Here's to your success,

Laurel D. Malvern

Chapter 1: The Importance of a Comprehensive Approach to Career Success

In the opening chapter of "The Road to Professional Excellence: A Holistic Guide to Career Success," Laurel D. Malvern sets the stage by emphasizing the critical importance of taking a comprehensive approach to achieving career success. This chapter serves as a foundational cornerstone, laying out the rationale for integrating various facets of personal development, professional skills, and strategic planning into a cohesive strategy.

Malvern explores how a fragmented approach to career advancement often leads to missed opportunities and unrealized potential. By contrast, she advocates for a holistic mindset that recognizes the interconnectedness of skills such as goal setting, communication proficiency, and leadership development. Readers are encouraged to view their career trajectories not as isolated events but as continuous journeys of growth and refinement.

Through compelling insights and practical examples, Malvern illustrates how embracing a holistic approach can enhance one's ability to navigate challenges, seize opportunities, and ultimately achieve long-term professional fulfillment. This chapter sets the tone for the rest of the book, promising a comprehensive guide that equips readers with the tools and strategies necessary to excel in today's competitive and rapidly evolving professional landscape.

Chapter 2: Laying the Foundation - Career Advice and Professional Development

In Chapter 2 of "The Road to Professional Excellence: A Holistic Guide to Career Success," Laurel D. Malvern delves into the essential elements of laying a solid foundation for career growth. This chapter serves as a vital starting point, offering invaluable advice and actionable insights aimed at individuals looking to establish a robust framework for their professional journey.

Malvern emphasizes the importance of understanding the fundamentals of career planning and development. She explores how strategic career decisions and continuous learning are crucial for staying relevant and advancing in today's competitive job market. Readers are guided through the process of creating personalized professional development plans tailored to their unique aspirations and skill sets.

Furthermore, the chapter addresses the significance of embracing a proactive approach to learning and skill acquisition. Malvern underscores the value of seeking out mentors, leveraging resources, and identifying opportunities for growth within one's current role or industry. By fostering a mindset of ongoing improvement and adaptation, readers can position themselves for long-term success and fulfillment in their careers.

Through practical examples and real-world scenarios, Malvern empowers readers to take charge of their professional trajectories with confidence and purpose. Chapter 2 sets the stage for subsequent chapters, promising a comprehensive exploration of key strategies and principles essential for navigating the complexities of modern-day career advancement.

Chapter 3: Professional Development

Welcome to Chapter 3 of "The Road to Professional Excellence: A Holistic Guide to Career Success." Here, we delve into the crucial steps needed to establish a strong foundation for your career journey. This chapter is designed to provide you with detailed insights and actionable advice that will empower you to navigate the complexities of career growth with confidence.

First and foremost, we emphasize the importance of strategic career planning. It's essential to align your personal aspirations with your professional goals to ensure clarity and direction. By assessing your skills, interests, and values, you can identify career paths that resonate deeply with who you are and where you want to go.

Continuous learning and development are also central to laying a solid foundation. In today's rapidly evolving job market, staying updated with industry trends and acquiring new skills is crucial. We explore how adopting a mindset of lifelong learning not only enhances your capabilities but also positions you as a proactive and adaptable professional.

Creating a personalized professional development plan is another key focus of this chapter. We guide you through the process of setting SMART goals—specific, measurable, achievable, relevant, and time-bound—and provide strategies for monitoring your progress. This proactive approach ensures that you're continually advancing towards your career objectives.

Moreover, we discuss the invaluable role of mentorship and networking. Seeking guidance from experienced mentors and building a strong professional network can provide you with invaluable insights and opportunities for growth. These relationships can open doors to new possibilities and help you navigate challenges more effectively.

Throughout this chapter, you'll find practical examples, case studies, and actionable tips that illustrate how to implement these strategies in your own career journey. By laying a solid foundation now, you'll set yourself up for long-term success and fulfillment in your chosen profession.

As you read through Chapter 2, consider how you can apply these insights to your own circumstances. Whether you're just starting out or looking to advance in your current career path, the principles discussed here will equip you with the knowledge and tools needed to build a resilient and thriving career.

Stay engaged, take notes, and reflect on how each concept resonates with your goals. Remember, your career journey is uniquely yours, and by laying a strong foundation today, you're paving the way for a successful and fulfilling future.

Firstly, strategic career planning involves a deliberate and systematic approach to mapping out your career trajectory. It starts with a thorough assessment of three key aspects:

Skills: Evaluating your skills involves identifying your strengths, competencies, and areas where you excel. This assessment helps you understand what you bring to the table professionally and where you can add the most value in your chosen field or industry.

Interests: Understanding your interests entails recognizing what activities, subjects, or types of work energize and engage you. By aligning your career with your interests, you increase your motivation and enjoyment in your job, leading to greater job satisfaction and longevity in your career.

Values: Assessing your values means identifying the principles, beliefs, and priorities that are most important to you in your work and life. Values guide your decision-making process, helping you choose opportunities and career paths that align with your ethical standards and personal fulfillment.

By conducting a comprehensive assessment of these three areas—skills, interests, and values—you gain clarity about your professional identity and career aspirations. This clarity is crucial for setting meaningful career goals and making informed decisions about your professional development.

Moreover, aligning your personal aspirations with your professional goals ensures coherence and direction in your career path. When your career goals resonate with your personal values and interests, you are more likely to stay motivated, committed, and focused on achieving your objectives. This alignment also helps you navigate career transitions, setbacks, and opportunities with resilience and purpose.

In essence, strategic career planning is not just about setting goals—it's about crafting a roadmap that integrates your strengths, passions, and principles into a cohesive career strategy. It empowers you to build a fulfilling and successful career that aligns with who you are and where you want to go professionally, ensuring sustained growth and satisfaction in your professional life.

Continuous learning and development are fundamental components of laying a solid foundation for career success. In today's rapidly evolving workplace, industries are constantly changing due to technological advancements, market shifts, and evolving customer expectations. Professionals who embrace a mindset of lifelong learning are better equipped to navigate these changes effectively and maintain relevance in their fields.

Here are key reasons why continuous learning is crucial:

Adaptability: The ability to adapt to new technologies, methodologies, and industry trends is essential for remaining competitive. Continuous learning allows professionals to stay abreast of emerging trends and adapt their skills and knowledge accordingly.

Skill Enhancement: Acquiring new skills and knowledge through ongoing learning programs enhances professional capabilities. This not only expands your expertise but also enables you to take on new responsibilities and tackle complex challenges with confidence.

Career Advancement: Employers value employees who demonstrate a commitment to learning and development. Continuous learners are often considered for promotions, leadership roles, and challenging assignments due to their proactive approach to skill enhancement.

Innovation: Lifelong learners are more likely to generate innovative ideas and solutions. Exposure to diverse perspectives and continuous education fosters creativity and problem-solving abilities, driving organizational innovation and growth.

Personal Fulfillment: Engaging in continuous learning contributes to personal satisfaction and professional fulfillment. It allows individuals to pursue their interests, deepen their expertise, and achieve career goals aligned with their passions and values.

Adopting a mindset of lifelong learning involves proactive steps such as attending workshops, pursuing certifications, participating in online courses, reading industry publications, and networking with peers. These activities not only keep professionals current in their fields but also demonstrate their commitment to personal and professional growth.

In summary, continuous learning and development are critical for laying a solid foundation in today's competitive job market. By embracing lifelong learning, professionals enhance their capabilities, adaptability, and career prospects, positioning themselves as valuable assets to employers and leaders in their industries.

Creating a personalized professional development plan is pivotal for professionals aiming to achieve sustained growth and success in their careers. In Chapter 2 of "The Road to Professional Excellence: A Holistic Guide to Career Success," we emphasize the importance of this strategic process and guide readers through the steps involved.

Setting SMART Goals: The foundation of a professional development plan lies in setting SMART goals—Specific, Measurable, Achievable, Relevant, and Time-bound. Specific goals clearly define what you want to accomplish, while measurable goals establish criteria for tracking progress. Achievable goals are realistic within your current capabilities and resources, and relevant goals align with your career aspirations. Time-bound goals have a defined timeframe for completion, providing a sense of urgency and accountability.

Identifying Development Areas: Assessing your current skills, competencies, and areas for improvement is essential. This self-assessment helps you identify gaps in knowledge or experience that need to be addressed to progress in your career. By pinpointing these development areas, you can tailor your professional development plan to focus on acquiring specific skills or gaining relevant experiences.

Strategies for Skill Enhancement: Once goals and development areas are identified, the next step is to outline strategies for achieving them. This may include enrolling in courses or certifications, seeking mentorship or coaching, attending workshops or conferences, and actively seeking out challenging assignments or projects at work. Each strategy should be aligned with your SMART goals and contribute to your overall career advancement.

Monitoring Progress: Effective professional development plans include mechanisms for monitoring progress towards your goals. Regularly reviewing your objectives and tracking milestones allows you to assess your development journey objectively. It enables you to celebrate successes, identify areas needing adjustment, and maintain momentum towards achieving your career objectives.

Adjusting and Adapting: Flexibility is crucial in professional development planning. As circumstances change or new opportunities arise, you may need to adjust your goals or strategies accordingly. This adaptive approach ensures that your plan remains relevant and responsive to both personal growth and evolving industry demands.

By creating a personalized professional development plan grounded in SMART goals and supported by strategic actions, individuals can proactively manage their career paths. This structured approach not only enhances professional skills and capabilities but also fosters a sense of empowerment and direction in achieving long-term career success.

Mentorship and networking are integral components of career growth and success, facilitating invaluable insights, opportunities, and support throughout one's professional journey. Here's how they contribute significantly:

Guidance and Insights: Mentors, typically seasoned professionals in your field, offer guidance based on their extensive experience and expertise. They provide valuable insights into industry trends, best practices, and potential career paths. Mentors can also offer personalized advice on navigating challenges, making critical decisions, and capitalizing on opportunities that arise in your career.

Skill Development: Mentorship goes beyond knowledge-sharing; it often involves skill development through hands-on learning and feedback. Mentors may provide opportunities for you to expand your skills, take on new responsibilities, or refine your approach to problem-solving and decision-making. This direct mentorship accelerates your professional growth and enhances your capabilities.

Networking Opportunities: Building a strong professional network opens doors to new opportunities and collaborations. Networking allows you to connect with peers, industry leaders, potential employers, and clients. These connections can lead to job referrals, partnerships, mentorship opportunities, and access to insider knowledge about job openings and career advancements.

Career Advancement: Effective networking and mentorship relationships can significantly impact your career advancement. By cultivating relationships with influential individuals in your industry, you increase your visibility and credibility. These relationships may lead to promotions, leadership roles, or invitations to participate in high-profile projects or initiatives.

Support and Encouragement: Both mentors and professional networks provide a support system that helps you navigate challenges and setbacks. They offer encouragement, constructive feedback, and perspectives that broaden your understanding of professional dynamics and enhance your resilience in the face of adversity.

In summary, mentorship and networking are not just about making connections — they are strategic investments in your professional development. By actively seeking out mentors and building a diverse professional network, you create opportunities for continuous learning, career advancement, and personal growth. These relationships enrich your career journey, helping you achieve your goals more effectively while contributing to your long-term success and satisfaction in your chosen field.

Example 1: Strategic Career Planning

Case Study: Sarah, a marketing professional, conducts a self-assessment of her skills (digital marketing, content creation) and interests (consumer behavior, social media trends). She aligns these with her value for creativity and impact.
Actionable Tip: Sarah sets a SMART goal to transition from a generalist to a specialist in social media marketing within the next year, focusing on measurable metrics like engagement rates and campaign ROI.

Example 2: Continuous Learning and Development

Case Study: John, an IT project manager, attends industry conferences and online courses regularly to stay updated on emerging technologies (e.g., AI, cybersecurity).
Actionable Tip: John sets aside dedicated time each month to learn a new programming language or project management methodology, ensuring he remains competitive in his field.

Example 3: Creating a Professional Development Plan

Case Study: Maria, a healthcare administrator, identifies leadership skills as a development area. She sets a SMART goal to complete a leadership training program within six months.
Actionable Tip: Maria schedules regular check-ins with her supervisor and mentor to review her progress, seek feedback, and adjust her plan as needed to stay on track toward her career objectives.

Example 4: Mentorship and Networking

Case Study: Tom, a young engineer, seeks mentorship from a senior colleague who provides guidance on navigating project challenges and career growth opportunities within the company.

Actionable Tip: Tom attends industry networking events and connects with professionals on LinkedIn, expanding his network and learning about job openings and industry trends.
Example 5: Personalized Professional Growth

Case Study: Emily, a business analyst, creates a professional development plan that includes attending workshops on data analytics and obtaining a certification in project management.
Actionable Tip: Emily joins a professional association related to her field, where she participates in webinars and discussion forums to enhance her knowledge and network with peers for career advancement opportunities.

By incorporating these practical examples, case studies, and actionable tips into their career journeys, readers can effectively lay a solid foundation for long-term success and fulfillment in their professions. Each strategy is designed to empower individuals to proactively manage their careers, adapt to industry changes, and capitalize on growth opportunities, ultimately achieving their professional goals with confidence and purpose.

Chapter 4: Understanding the Fundamentals of Career Planning

In Chapter 4 of "The Road to Professional Excellence: A Holistic Guide to Career Success," we delve into the essential principles of career planning, providing a comprehensive framework to help you navigate your professional journey effectively.

Assessing Your Current Position: The chapter begins by encouraging readers to conduct a thorough assessment of their current career status. This involves evaluating your skills, experiences, and accomplishments to gain a clear understanding of where you stand in your career path.

Setting Clear and Achievable Goals: We emphasize the importance of setting specific and achievable career goals. Whether it's aiming for a promotion, transitioning to a new industry, or acquiring specialized skills, defining clear objectives provides direction and motivation.

Identifying Career Options: Readers are guided through strategies to explore and evaluate various career options. This includes researching industries, networking with professionals in different fields, and considering how their skills and interests align with potential career paths.

Creating a Career Action Plan: Developing a structured career action plan is essential. This involves outlining the steps and timelines needed to achieve your career goals. By breaking down larger objectives into manageable tasks, you can track progress and make adjustments as needed.

Adapting to Change: Recognizing that career planning is dynamic, we discuss the importance of flexibility and adaptability. This includes being open to new opportunities, reassessing goals based on changing circumstances, and continuously updating your skills to stay relevant in the job market.

Throughout Chapter 4, practical examples, case studies, and actionable insights illustrate how to apply these principles in real-world scenarios. By understanding the fundamentals of career planning and proactively managing your professional trajectory, you can enhance your career satisfaction, achieve personal growth, and navigate towards long-term success in your chosen field.

Assessing your current position in your career is a foundational step towards effective career planning and development. As an expert, here's how this process unfolds and its significance:

Evaluating Skills: Start by taking stock of your skills and competencies. Identify your strengths — areas where you excel and have a proven track record. This evaluation helps you understand what unique abilities you bring to the table and how they contribute to your professional identity.

Assessing Experiences: Reflect on your professional experiences, including previous roles, projects, and responsibilities. Consider the skills you've acquired, challenges you've overcome, and achievements you've accomplished. Evaluating these experiences provides insights into your career trajectory and highlights areas where you may need further development.

Reviewing Accomplishments: Take inventory of your accomplishments and milestones. These could include tangible outcomes such as successful projects, awards, promotions, or recognition for your contributions. Assessing your accomplishments not only boosts confidence but also reinforces your capabilities and areas of expertise.

Identifying Areas for Growth: Through this assessment, identify areas where you may have gaps in skills or experiences that are crucial for advancing in your career. This self-awareness helps you prioritize areas for development and sets the stage for setting meaningful career goals.

Gaining Clarity and Direction: By conducting a thorough assessment of your skills, experiences, and accomplishments, you gain a clear understanding of your current career position. This clarity enables you to make informed decisions about your career path, such as pursuing opportunities that align with your strengths or addressing areas needing improvement.

Strategic Career Planning: Armed with this self-assessment, you can develop a strategic career plan that leverages your strengths and addresses areas for growth. This plan serves as a roadmap for setting specific career goals, identifying necessary actions, and monitoring progress towards achieving your objectives.

Overall, assessing your current career position is not just about evaluating where you are now; it's about gaining insights that empower you to take proactive steps towards your desired future. This process sets the foundation for effective career planning, personal growth, and ultimately, achieving long-term success in your professional endeavors.

Setting clear and achievable career goals is a critical aspect of effective career planning and advancement. Here's why it's essential and how to approach it:

Direction and Focus: Clear goals provide a roadmap for your career journey. They define where you want to go and what steps you need to take to get there. Whether your goal is to advance within your current role, transition to a new industry, or acquire specific skills, having a clear objective keeps you focused and motivated.

Clarity in Decision-Making: When you have defined goals, you can make informed decisions about opportunities that align with your career aspirations. This clarity helps you prioritize tasks, allocate resources effectively, and stay committed to achieving your objectives amidst competing demands.

Motivation and Engagement: Setting specific goals creates a sense of purpose and motivation. It gives you something tangible to work towards, boosting your enthusiasm and dedication to professional growth. Achieving smaller milestones along the way reinforces your progress and encourages continued effort.

Measurable Progress: Clear goals are measurable, allowing you to track your progress and celebrate achievements. This measurement helps you assess how far you've come and adjust your strategies if necessary to stay on course towards your ultimate career objectives.

Achievability and Realism: Goals should be achievable within a realistic timeframe and align with your current capabilities and resources. This ensures that you set yourself up for success rather than frustration. Break larger goals into smaller, manageable tasks to maintain momentum and build confidence as you progress.

Flexibility and Adaptability: While goals provide direction, it's important to remain flexible. External factors or personal growth may necessitate adjustments to your goals over time. Flexibility allows you to respond to changing circumstances while staying committed to your overarching career aspirations.

In practical terms, setting clear and achievable goals involves:

Defining Specific Objectives: Clearly articulate what you want to accomplish, such as obtaining a promotion within the next year or acquiring certification in a new technology.
Establishing Measurable Outcomes: Identify metrics or criteria to assess progress and success, such as performance evaluations, completion of training programs, or achieving specific milestones.
Setting Realistic Timelines: Determine a timeline that balances ambition with feasibility, considering external factors like industry trends, personal commitments, and professional development opportunities.
Creating an Action Plan: Outline actionable steps and strategies to reach your goals, including acquiring necessary skills, expanding your network, and seeking mentorship or guidance.

By emphasizing the importance of setting clear and achievable career goals, individuals can effectively navigate their professional paths with purpose, resilience, and continuous growth. This approach not only enhances career satisfaction but also positions individuals to seize opportunities and achieve long-term success in their chosen fields.

Identifying career options is a crucial step in career planning that allows individuals to explore and evaluate various paths aligned with their skills, interests, and aspirations. Here's how this process unfolds and its significance:

Researching Industries and Trends: Begin by conducting thorough research into different industries and sectors of interest. Explore factors such as growth projections, job demand, emerging technologies, and economic trends. Understanding industry landscapes helps you assess where opportunities lie and which sectors align best with your career goals.

Networking and Informational Interviews: Networking with professionals in different fields provides valuable insights into various career options. Engage with industry experts, attend networking events, and seek informational interviews to gather firsthand knowledge about roles, responsibilities, and career trajectories within specific industries or companies. These interactions offer perspectives that may not be apparent through research alone.

Assessing Skills and Interests: Reflect on your own skills, strengths, and interests. Consider what tasks or activities energize you, where you excel, and what values are important to you in a career. Aligning your skills and interests with potential career paths increases the likelihood of finding fulfilling and rewarding opportunities that resonate with who you are professionally.

Exploring Alternative Paths: Career exploration involves considering alternative paths or roles that leverage your transferable skills and experiences. For example, professionals from diverse backgrounds may pivot into related fields by highlighting their adaptable skills and demonstrating how these can add value in new contexts.

Considering Career Development Opportunities: Evaluate opportunities for career growth and advancement within chosen fields. Identify pathways for skill development, certifications, advanced degrees, or specialized training that can enhance your qualifications and expand your career options over time.

Making Informed Decisions: Armed with research, networking insights, and a clear understanding of your own strengths and interests, you can make informed decisions about which career options align best with your long-term goals and personal aspirations. This informed approach minimizes uncertainty and enhances your ability to pursue opportunities that offer both professional fulfillment and growth.

In practical terms, identifying career options involves proactive steps such as:

Conducting Market Research: Using resources like industry reports, job market analyses, and professional associations to gather data on current trends and opportunities.
Networking Effectively: Building relationships with professionals through platforms like LinkedIn, attending industry events, and participating in professional organizations.
Seeking Mentorship: Engaging with mentors who can provide guidance and advice based on their own career experiences.
Self-Assessment: Continuously assessing and updating your skills, interests, and career goals to stay aligned with evolving industry demands and personal aspirations.

By guiding readers through strategies to explore and evaluate career options, individuals can navigate their career paths with confidence, resilience, and a proactive mindset. This approach not only enhances career satisfaction but also positions individuals to capitalize on opportunities for professional growth and success in dynamic and competitive job markets.

Creating a career action plan is a strategic process that enables individuals to map out their career goals, outline actionable steps, and monitor progress effectively. Here's why it's essential and how to approach it:

Clarity and Focus: A career action plan provides clarity by defining specific objectives and the necessary steps to achieve them. It ensures that your career goals are well-defined, measurable, and aligned with your long-term aspirations. This clarity helps maintain focus amidst daily responsibilities and distractions.

Strategic Goal Setting: Start by identifying your career goals—whether it's securing a promotion, transitioning to a new role or industry, acquiring specific skills, or starting a business. These goals should be SMART (Specific, Measurable, Achievable, Relevant, Time-bound) to provide a clear roadmap for success.

Breaking Down Objectives: Break down larger career objectives into smaller, manageable tasks or milestones. This approach makes daunting goals more achievable by dividing them into actionable steps that you can tackle incrementally.

Setting Timelines: Establish realistic timelines for each task or milestone within your action plan. Timelines create accountability and urgency, motivating you to stay on track and make steady progress towards your career goals.

Resource Allocation: Determine the resources needed to achieve each task, such as time, finances, training, or networking opportunities. Allocating resources strategically ensures that you have the necessary support and tools to succeed.

Monitoring and Evaluation: Regularly monitor your progress against the milestones outlined in your action plan. Track accomplishments, identify areas where adjustments may be needed, and celebrate achievements along the way. This continuous evaluation allows you to adapt to changing circumstances and refine your approach as necessary.

Flexibility and Adaptability: Remain flexible in your career action plan. External factors, unexpected opportunities, or personal growth may require adjustments to timelines or strategies. Being adaptable allows you to navigate challenges effectively and capitalize on emerging opportunities.

Seeking Support and Feedback: Engage mentors, peers, or career coaches who can provide guidance, feedback, and support as you execute your career action plan. Their insights can offer valuable perspectives and help you overcome obstacles more efficiently.

Practical steps in creating a career action plan include:

Identifying Short-Term and Long-Term Goals: Clearly define what you want to achieve in the near future and over the course of your career.
Outlining Specific Actions: Detail the specific actions or tasks required to achieve each goal, ensuring they are actionable and realistic.
Establishing Milestones: Break down goals into measurable milestones with deadlines to track progress effectively.
Regular Review and Adjustment: Schedule regular reviews to assess progress, adjust timelines or strategies as needed, and set new objectives as you achieve milestones.

By developing and executing a well-crafted career action plan, individuals can proactively manage their professional development, maximize opportunities for advancement, and ultimately achieve long-term career success and fulfillment. This structured approach empowers individuals to take control of their careers and navigate the complexities of today's competitive job market with confidence.

Adapting to change is a crucial skill in career planning and development, especially in today's rapidly evolving job market. As an expert, here's why flexibility and adaptability are essential and how individuals can cultivate these qualities:

Embracing New Opportunities: The job market and industry landscapes are constantly evolving with technological advancements, economic shifts, and changing consumer behaviors. Being open to new opportunities allows individuals to capitalize on emerging trends, explore different career paths, and remain agile in their professional pursuits.

Reassessing Goals: Recognizing that circumstances can change, it's important to periodically reassess career goals and objectives. This involves evaluating whether current career trajectories align with personal aspirations, industry demands, and professional growth opportunities. Adjusting goals ensures relevance and allows individuals to pivot when necessary to stay on track towards long-term success.

Continuous Skills Development: To stay competitive in the job market, individuals must continuously update and expand their skill set. This proactive approach involves acquiring new skills, certifications, or knowledge relevant to current industry trends and job requirements. It also includes honing soft skills such as adaptability, communication, and problem-solving, which are increasingly valued by employers.

Networking and Building Relationships: Maintaining a robust professional network provides access to diverse perspectives, mentorship, and potential career opportunities. Networking allows individuals to stay informed about industry developments, gather insights from peers and experts, and leverage connections for career advancement or job transitions.

Resilience and Growth Mindset: Adapting to change requires resilience—a mindset that embraces challenges as opportunities for growth. Individuals with a growth mindset view setbacks as learning experiences and are willing to step outside their comfort zones to pursue new opportunities or overcome obstacles.

Monitoring Industry Trends: Keeping abreast of industry trends, market demands, and technological advancements is essential for proactive career planning. This knowledge enables individuals to anticipate changes, identify emerging opportunities, and position themselves as valuable contributors in their respective fields.

Practical steps to adapt to change include:

Continual Learning: Enroll in courses, workshops, or online programs to acquire new skills or deepen existing knowledge.
Networking: Engage in professional associations, attend industry conferences, and build relationships with peers and mentors.
Flexible Career Planning: Regularly review and update your career action plan based on personal growth, industry shifts, or changes in career goals.
Embracing Innovation: Seek out opportunities to innovate, collaborate on cross-functional projects, and contribute to organizational initiatives that align with your career objectives.
By fostering flexibility, adaptability, and a proactive approach to career planning, individuals can navigate uncertainties, seize opportunities, and achieve sustainable career growth and fulfillment. Embracing change as an integral part of professional development empowers individuals to thrive in dynamic and competitive environments, positioning them for long-term success in their chosen careers.

Chapter 5: Importance of Continuous Learning and Development

In Chapter 5 of "The Road to Professional Excellence: A Holistic Guide to Career Success," we explore the fundamental role of continuous learning and development in achieving long-term career growth and professional fulfillment.

Adapting to Evolving Industries: Industries today are marked by rapid advancements in technology and changing market dynamics. Continuous learning equips individuals with the knowledge and skills needed to adapt to these changes effectively. It ensures that professionals remain relevant and competitive in their respective fields.

Enhancing Professional Competence: Learning is a lifelong journey that enhances professional competence and expertise. By acquiring new knowledge, mastering emerging technologies, and staying updated on industry trends, individuals can broaden their skill sets and improve their performance in current roles.

Staying Ahead of the Curve: Proactive learning allows individuals to anticipate future trends and challenges. It empowers them to innovate, identify opportunities for growth, and position themselves as leaders and influencers within their organizations or industries.

Personal and Career Development: Continuous learning fosters personal growth and career advancement. It enables individuals to pursue new career paths, take on leadership roles, and achieve their professional aspirations. Investing in education and skill development demonstrates commitment to ongoing improvement and excellence.

Building Resilience and Adaptability: Learning new skills cultivates resilience and adaptability, essential traits in navigating career transitions and overcoming obstacles. It equips individuals with the confidence to embrace change, tackle challenges, and seize opportunities for advancement.

Fostering a Culture of Learning: Organizations benefit from employees who prioritize continuous learning. They contribute to a culture of innovation, knowledge sharing, and continuous improvement. Employees who engage in professional development are more motivated, engaged, and capable of driving organizational success.

Practical strategies for continuous learning and development include:

Formal Education: Pursuing advanced degrees, certifications, or specialized courses related to your field.
Informal Learning: Engaging in self-study, reading industry publications, or participating in webinars and online forums.
Skill Enhancement: Attending workshops, seminars, or training sessions to acquire new skills or enhance existing ones.
Mentorship and Coaching: Seeking guidance from mentors, coaches, or industry experts to gain insights and advice for professional growth.

By emphasizing the importance of continuous learning and development, individuals can proactively manage their career trajectories, adapt to industry changes, and achieve sustainable success in today's dynamic and competitive job market. This chapter serves as a guide for fostering a mindset of lifelong learning and leveraging educational opportunities to maximize professional potential and personal fulfillment.

Adapting to evolving industries is crucial in today's dynamic economic landscape, where rapid advancements in technology and shifting market dynamics redefine professional requirements. Here's why continuous learning is essential for individuals aiming to stay relevant and competitive:

Navigating Technological Advancements: Industries are increasingly reliant on technological innovations. Continuous learning enables professionals to acquire proficiency in new technologies, software, and digital tools essential for optimizing workflows, enhancing productivity, and delivering innovative solutions. This adaptability ensures that individuals can leverage emerging technologies to maintain efficiency and competitiveness.

Responding to Market Changes: Markets evolve in response to consumer preferences, economic trends, and global events. Professionals need to stay informed about market shifts, regulatory changes, and emerging trends to anticipate industry demands and adjust strategies accordingly. Continuous learning equips individuals with insights and skills to identify opportunities, mitigate risks, and align business practices with evolving market dynamics.

Enhancing Professional Competence: Learning fosters continuous improvement of skills, knowledge, and competencies. Professionals who engage in ongoing education and skill development demonstrate a commitment to professional growth and excellence. This proactive approach not only enhances individual capabilities but also positions professionals as valued contributors capable of addressing complex challenges and driving organizational success.

Adopting a Growth Mindset: Continuous learning cultivates a growth mindset—a belief in one's ability to learn and adapt. This mindset encourages resilience, curiosity, and openness to new ideas and perspectives. Professionals with a growth mindset are more adaptable to change, more willing to experiment with innovative solutions, and more adept at seizing opportunities for personal and professional development.

Remaining Competitive in the Job Market: In a competitive job market, continuous learning distinguishes candidates who are proactive in staying updated and relevant. Employers prioritize candidates with a commitment to ongoing professional development and a willingness to evolve alongside industry trends. Continuous learners are better equipped to pursue career advancement opportunities, negotiate competitive salaries, and secure roles aligned with their skills and aspirations.

Practical strategies for adapting to evolving industries through continuous learning include:

Enrolling in Courses and Workshops: Attending seminars, workshops, and online courses to acquire new skills and knowledge relevant to current industry trends.
Networking and Collaboration: Engaging with peers, mentors, and industry professionals to exchange insights, share best practices, and stay informed about emerging developments.
Reading Industry Publications: Regularly reading industry journals, reports, and publications to stay abreast of technological innovations, market trends, and regulatory changes.
Participating in Professional Associations: Joining professional associations and attending conferences to network with industry leaders, participate in discussions, and gain exposure to cutting-edge practices.

By embracing continuous learning as a cornerstone of professional development, individuals can adapt to evolving industries, enhance their professional competence, and position themselves as indispensable contributors in today's rapidly changing business environment.

Enhancing professional competence through lifelong learning is essential for individuals seeking to excel in their careers and remain competitive in today's dynamic professional landscape. Here's why continuous learning is crucial for expanding skills and expertise:

Adapting to Industry Changes: Industries evolve rapidly due to technological advancements, market shifts, and regulatory updates. Continuous learning enables professionals to stay updated on emerging trends, best practices, and industry standards. This adaptability ensures that individuals can anticipate changes, pivot strategies, and leverage new opportunities effectively.

Mastering Emerging Technologies: Technology plays a pivotal role in modern workplaces. Continuous learning allows professionals to acquire proficiency in new tools, software, and digital platforms relevant to their industries. By mastering emerging technologies, individuals enhance efficiency, streamline processes, and innovate solutions that drive business growth and competitiveness.

Broadening Skill Sets: Lifelong learning enables professionals to diversify their skill sets beyond their core competencies. By exploring new disciplines, acquiring complementary skills, and expanding knowledge areas, individuals become versatile contributors capable of tackling multidimensional challenges and assuming diverse roles within their organizations.

Improving Performance and Productivity: Acquiring new knowledge and skills enhances professional capabilities, leading to improved performance in current roles. Individuals who continually update their expertise are better equipped to solve complex problems, make informed decisions, and achieve measurable results that contribute to organizational success.

Promoting Career Advancement: Employers value employees who invest in their professional development and demonstrate a commitment to learning. Continuous learners are more likely to be considered for promotions, leadership opportunities, and strategic projects that align with their enhanced skill sets and demonstrated expertise.

Fostering Innovation and Creativity: Learning fosters a mindset of innovation and creativity by exposing individuals to diverse perspectives, methodologies, and problem-solving approaches. Professionals who engage in continuous learning are more inclined to generate innovative ideas, adapt novel solutions, and drive initiatives that push organizational boundaries.

Practical steps for enhancing professional competence through lifelong learning include:

Formal Education: Pursuing advanced degrees, certifications, or specialized courses relevant to career goals and industry demands.
Self-Directed Learning: Engaging in self-study through online courses, webinars, tutorials, and educational resources to explore new topics or deepen existing knowledge.
On-the-Job Training: Participating in workshops, seminars, and professional development programs offered by employers to enhance specific skills and competencies.
Networking and Mentorship: Leveraging relationships with mentors, peers, and industry experts to exchange knowledge, seek guidance, and gain insights into emerging trends and practices.

By embracing lifelong learning as a cornerstone of professional growth, individuals not only enhance their competence and expertise but also position themselves as proactive contributors capable of driving innovation, adaptation, and sustainable success in their careers.

Staying ahead of the curve through proactive learning is vital for professionals aiming to maintain a competitive edge and drive success in their careers. Here's an expert explanation of why this approach is essential and how it can be effectively implemented:

Anticipating Future Trends: Proactive learning involves staying informed about emerging trends, technological advancements, and shifts in market dynamics. By continually updating their knowledge, professionals can anticipate changes before they become widespread. This foresight allows individuals to prepare for future challenges and opportunities, ensuring they remain relevant and valuable in their fields.

Driving Innovation: Innovation stems from the ability to think ahead and develop new solutions to existing problems. Proactive learners are often exposed to cutting-edge ideas and technologies, enabling them to bring fresh perspectives and innovative approaches to their work. This mindset fosters a culture of creativity and continuous improvement within organizations.

Identifying Growth Opportunities: Proactive learning helps professionals recognize potential areas for growth and expansion. By understanding industry trends and customer needs, individuals can identify new markets, products, or services that align with their organization's strengths. This strategic insight positions them to capitalize on emerging opportunities and contribute to their organization's success.

Becoming Leaders and Influencers: Professionals who prioritize continuous learning often develop a reputation for expertise and forward-thinking. This positions them as leaders and influencers within their organizations and industries. Their proactive approach demonstrates a commitment to excellence and a readiness to guide others through changes and advancements.

Enhancing Strategic Decision-Making: Staying ahead of the curve involves making informed decisions based on current and anticipated trends. Proactive learners are better equipped to analyze data, forecast outcomes, and devise strategies that align with future scenarios. This strategic decision-making capability is highly valued in leadership roles and critical for organizational success.

Building a Competitive Advantage: Organizations thrive when their employees are knowledgeable and adaptable. Proactive learning equips professionals with skills and insights that differentiate them from their peers. This competitive advantage not only enhances individual career prospects but also strengthens the organization's position in the marketplace.

Practical strategies for staying ahead of the curve through proactive learning include:

Continuous Education: Regularly enrolling in courses, certifications, and professional development programs to stay updated on the latest industry developments.
Industry Research: Actively researching and monitoring industry reports, market analyses, and technological innovations to identify trends and predict their impact.

Professional Networking: Engaging with industry peers, attending conferences, and participating in professional associations to exchange knowledge and stay connected with thought leaders.

Mentorship and Collaboration: Seeking mentorship from experienced professionals and collaborating with colleagues on innovative projects to gain diverse perspectives and insights.

Experimentation and Innovation: Encouraging a culture of experimentation within the organization, where new ideas are tested and refined to drive innovation and growth.

By embracing proactive learning, professionals can anticipate and adapt to changes, drive innovation, and position themselves as strategic leaders in their fields. This forward-thinking approach ensures long-term career success and contributes to the sustained growth and competitiveness of their organizations.

Continuous learning is a powerful catalyst for both personal and career development. It fosters growth, opens new opportunities, and empowers individuals to achieve their professional aspirations. Here's an expert explanation of how continuous learning impacts personal and career development:

Personal Growth:
Self-Improvement: Continuous learning encourages self-improvement by helping individuals expand their knowledge base, develop new skills, and refine existing ones. This ongoing process contributes to a deeper understanding of one's strengths and areas for development, leading to personal fulfillment and confidence.
Adaptability and Resilience: Learning new skills and concepts enhances an individual's ability to adapt to changing circumstances. This adaptability fosters resilience, enabling professionals to navigate challenges, overcome obstacles, and thrive in dynamic environments.
Intellectual Stimulation: Engaging in continuous learning keeps the mind active and stimulated. It promotes critical thinking, problem-solving, and creativity, which are essential for both personal growth and professional success.
Enhanced Communication Skills: Learning often involves interacting with diverse groups and absorbing new perspectives, which can significantly improve communication skills. Effective communication is crucial for personal relationships and professional networking.
Career Advancement:
New Career Paths: Continuous learning opens doors to new career paths and opportunities. By acquiring new qualifications, certifications, or skills, individuals can pivot to different roles or industries, broadening their career prospects.

Leadership Development: To take on leadership roles, professionals need a diverse skill set that includes strategic thinking, people management, and decision-making. Continuous learning provides the tools and knowledge necessary to develop these leadership qualities and prepare for higher responsibilities.

Professional Aspirations: Achieving long-term professional goals often requires specialized knowledge and advanced skills. Continuous learning helps individuals stay on track to meet these aspirations by equipping them with the expertise needed to succeed in their chosen fields.

Commitment to Excellence: Investing in education and skill development demonstrates a commitment to continuous improvement and excellence. Employers value this dedication, as it reflects an individual's proactive approach to staying relevant and contributing to organizational success.

Practical Strategies for Continuous Learning:

Pursuing Advanced Education: Enroll in higher education programs, professional certifications, and specialized courses that align with career goals and industry demands.

Attending Workshops and Seminars: Participate in industry-specific workshops, conferences, and seminars to stay updated on the latest trends and best practices.

Online Learning Platforms: Utilize online learning platforms such as Coursera, Udemy, and LinkedIn Learning to access a wide range of courses and training programs.

Reading and Research: Regularly read industry publications, research papers, and books to deepen your knowledge and stay informed about new developments.

Networking and Mentorship: Build a network of mentors, peers, and industry experts who can provide guidance, share insights, and support your learning journey.

Examples of Continuous Learning in Action:

Transitioning Industries: An IT professional might take courses in cybersecurity to transition into a new, high-demand area within the tech industry.

Leadership Training: An aspiring manager might enroll in leadership development programs to build the necessary skills for a future executive role.

Skill Enhancement: A marketing specialist might take advanced analytics courses to improve their ability to interpret data and drive more effective campaigns.

By committing to continuous learning, individuals can foster both personal growth and career advancement, ensuring they remain competitive and fulfilled in an ever-changing professional landscape. This commitment to ongoing education not only enhances individual capabilities but also demonstrates a proactive approach to achieving excellence and success.

Building resilience and adaptability through continuous learning is critical for successfully navigating career transitions and overcoming professional challenges. Here's an expert explanation of how learning new skills fosters these essential traits and the impact they have on career development:

Resilience and Adaptability Defined:
Resilience is the ability to recover quickly from difficulties and setbacks. It involves maintaining a positive attitude and persevering through challenges.
Adaptability is the capacity to adjust to new conditions and changes in the environment. It includes being flexible and open to new ideas, processes, and ways of working.
The Role of Continuous Learning:
Embracing Change: Continuous learning encourages individuals to embrace change rather than fear it. By regularly acquiring new skills and knowledge, professionals become more comfortable with the idea of change and view it as an opportunity for growth rather than a threat.
Developing Problem-Solving Skills: Learning new skills often involves tackling complex problems and finding innovative solutions. This process enhances problem-solving abilities, which are crucial for overcoming obstacles and making informed decisions during career transitions.
Boosting Confidence: Gaining new competencies and expertise boosts self-confidence. When individuals feel confident in their abilities, they are more likely to take on new challenges, pursue ambitious goals, and navigate uncertainties with assurance.
Staying Relevant: The job market is constantly evolving, with new technologies and methodologies emerging regularly. Continuous learning ensures that professionals stay current with industry trends and developments, making them more adaptable to changing job requirements and career landscapes.

Expanding Career Opportunities: Acquiring new skills can open doors to diverse career opportunities. Whether it's a lateral move within the same industry or a complete career shift, continuous learning provides the versatility needed to explore different paths and seize new opportunities.

Practical Strategies for Building Resilience and Adaptability:

Lifelong Learning: Commit to a mindset of lifelong learning. Regularly seek out educational opportunities, whether through formal education, online courses, or self-directed study.

Embrace Challenges: View challenges as opportunities to learn and grow. Take on projects that push your limits and require you to develop new skills or approaches.

Seek Feedback: Actively seek feedback from colleagues, mentors, and supervisors. Constructive feedback helps identify areas for improvement and fosters a culture of continuous development.

Network and Collaborate: Engage with a diverse network of professionals. Collaboration and exposure to different perspectives can enhance adaptability and introduce new ways of thinking.

Practice Self-Care: Resilience is also about maintaining mental and emotional well-being. Practice self-care, manage stress effectively, and ensure a healthy work-life balance to sustain long-term adaptability.

Real-World Examples:

Career Transition: A mid-career professional in traditional marketing who learns digital marketing skills can transition to roles in the fast-growing field of digital marketing, thus staying relevant in the evolving job market.

Technological Adaptation: An engineer who continuously updates their knowledge about the latest software and automation technologies can adapt to changes in their industry, leading to career advancement and increased job security.

Leadership Development: A manager who engages in leadership training and develops emotional intelligence can better navigate organizational changes, lead teams effectively through transitions, and drive positive outcomes even in challenging circumstances.

By cultivating resilience and adaptability through continuous learning, professionals equip themselves to confidently face the dynamic nature of today's job market. These traits enable individuals to not only survive but thrive in the face of change, positioning them for sustained success and advancement in their careers.

Fostering a culture of learning within an organization is essential for cultivating an environment of innovation, knowledge sharing, and continuous improvement. Here's an expert explanation of why this is important and how it benefits both employees and the organization:

Benefits of a Learning Culture:
Innovation and Creativity: A culture of learning encourages employees to think outside the box and explore new ideas. Continuous learning exposes employees to diverse perspectives and emerging trends, fostering a mindset that embraces innovation and creative problem-solving.
Knowledge Sharing: When employees prioritize learning, they often share new insights and skills with their colleagues. This knowledge transfer enhances collective expertise, ensures best practices are widely adopted, and prevents knowledge silos.
Continuous Improvement: Organizations that promote learning create an environment where continuous improvement is the norm. Employees regularly seek ways to enhance their skills, streamline processes, and improve outcomes, leading to increased efficiency and effectiveness.
Employee Motivation and Engagement: Professional development opportunities are highly valued by employees. When organizations invest in their growth, employees feel appreciated and motivated. This leads to higher levels of job satisfaction, engagement, and loyalty.
Adaptability and Resilience: A learning culture prepares employees to adapt to changes and disruptions. They develop resilience through continuous skill development, enabling them to navigate challenges and contribute to the organization's agility and long-term success.
Talent Attraction and Retention: Organizations known for fostering a culture of learning are more attractive to top talent. Professionals seek out employers who support their development, making it easier for such organizations to attract and retain skilled employees.

Strategies to Foster a Culture of Learning:

Leadership Commitment: Leaders must champion continuous learning by setting an example and prioritizing their development. When leadership actively supports learning initiatives, it signals the importance of professional growth to the entire organization.

Provide Resources and Opportunities: Offer diverse learning opportunities such as workshops, seminars, online courses, and access to educational resources. Create pathways for employees to pursue certifications, advanced degrees, and skill-building programs.

Encourage Collaboration and Knowledge Sharing: Create platforms for employees to share knowledge and collaborate on learning projects. This can include mentorship programs, internal training sessions, and collaborative tools that facilitate information exchange.

Recognize and Reward Learning: Acknowledge employees who actively engage in learning and development. Recognition programs, career advancement opportunities, and incentives for completing training programs can motivate others to follow suit.

Create a Safe Learning Environment: Encourage experimentation and learning from failure. A culture that views mistakes as learning opportunities rather than setbacks promotes a willingness to take risks and innovate.

Integrate Learning into Daily Work: Embed learning opportunities into regular workflows. Encourage employees to dedicate time to learning during work hours and integrate new skills into their daily tasks and responsibilities.

Monitor and Assess Progress: Regularly evaluate the impact of learning initiatives on employee performance and organizational outcomes. Use feedback and assessments to refine and improve learning programs continuously.

Real-World Examples:

Google's 20% Time: Google encourages employees to spend 20% of their work time on projects that interest them, fostering creativity and innovation. This policy has led to the development of some of Google's most successful products.

LinkedIn's Learning Platform: LinkedIn provides employees with access to a vast library of online courses through LinkedIn Learning. This resource supports continuous skill development and professional growth.

Microsoft's Growth Mindset: Microsoft promotes a growth mindset culture, encouraging employees to embrace learning and development as core values. This approach has been instrumental in the company's successful transformation and innovation initiatives.

By fostering a culture of learning, organizations can drive innovation, enhance employee engagement, and ensure continuous improvement. This strategic focus on professional development not only benefits individual employees but also contributes to the overall success and competitiveness of the organization.

Practical Strategies for Continuous Learning and Development:

1. Formal Education:

Pursuing Advanced Degrees: Enroll in advanced degree programs such as a Master's or PhD that align with your career goals. Advanced degrees provide in-depth knowledge and can open doors to higher-level positions.

Certifications: Obtain professional certifications specific to your industry. For example, Project Management Professional (PMP) for project managers, Certified Public Accountant (CPA) for accountants, or Certified Information Systems Security Professional (CISSP) for cybersecurity professionals. Certifications validate your expertise and can enhance your credibility.

Specialized Courses: Take specialized courses that address specific skills or knowledge areas relevant to your field. Many universities and online platforms offer courses that allow you to stay current with industry trends and technologies.

2. Informal Learning:

Self-Study: Dedicate time to self-study by reading books, articles, and research papers related to your industry. This helps you stay informed about the latest developments and best practices.

Industry Publications: Subscribe to and regularly read industry journals, magazines, and newsletters. These publications provide valuable insights into emerging trends, innovations, and case studies.

Webinars and Online Forums: Participate in webinars and online forums to learn from experts and engage with peers. Platforms like Coursera, edX, and LinkedIn Learning offer webinars on a wide range of topics. Online forums such as Reddit, Stack Exchange, and professional LinkedIn groups provide opportunities for discussion and knowledge exchange.

3. Skill Enhancement:

Workshops and Seminars: Attend workshops and seminars to gain practical skills and hands-on experience. These events often feature industry leaders who provide training on the latest tools, techniques, and methodologies.

Training Sessions: Participate in company-sponsored training sessions or seek out external training programs. Many organizations offer in-house training to help employees develop new skills or enhance existing ones.

Professional Conferences: Attend professional conferences and trade shows. These events offer a mix of learning opportunities, including keynote speeches, breakout sessions, and networking opportunities.

4. Mentorship and Coaching:

Seeking Mentors: Find mentors within your organization or industry who can provide guidance, support, and advice. Mentors can share their experiences, offer feedback, and help you navigate your career path.

Coaching: Engage with professional coaches who specialize in career development. Coaches can help you set goals, develop strategies for achieving them, and provide accountability.

Industry Experts: Connect with industry experts through professional associations, networking events, and social media platforms. Experts can offer valuable insights into industry trends, challenges, and opportunities.

Practical Examples:

Formal Education Example: A software engineer pursues a Master's degree in Artificial Intelligence to specialize in machine learning and advance to a senior engineering role.

Informal Learning Example: A marketing professional regularly reads industry blogs, listens to marketing podcasts, and participates in LinkedIn groups to stay updated on digital marketing trends.

Skill Enhancement Example: An HR manager attends a workshop on advanced HR analytics to improve their ability to analyze workforce data and make data-driven decisions.

Mentorship and Coaching Example: A young entrepreneur seeks mentorship from a successful business owner to gain insights into scaling their startup and overcoming common challenges.

Implementing Continuous Learning:

Set Clear Learning Goals: Define what you want to achieve through continuous learning. Set specific, measurable, achievable, relevant, and time-bound (SMART) goals.

Create a Learning Plan: Develop a plan that outlines the steps you need to take to achieve your learning goals. Include both formal and informal learning activities.

Allocate Time: Dedicate regular time slots for learning activities. Consistency is key to making continuous learning a habit.

Evaluate Progress: Regularly assess your progress towards your learning goals. Adjust your plan as needed to stay on track.

Stay Curious: Cultivate a mindset of curiosity and openness to new ideas. Embrace the learning process and seek opportunities to expand your knowledge and skills.

By implementing these practical strategies for continuous learning and development, professionals can stay competitive, adapt to changes, and achieve long-term career success.

Chapter 6: Creating a Personalized Professional Development Plan

In this chapter, we delve into the critical process of creating a personalized professional development plan. A well-structured plan serves as a roadmap for your career, guiding you towards your professional goals and ensuring continuous growth and improvement. Here's how to develop an effective plan:

Assessing Your Current Position
Before you can plan for the future, you need to understand where you stand today. Begin by conducting a thorough self-assessment:

Evaluate Your Skills: List your current skills and rate your proficiency in each. Identify areas where you excel and areas where you need improvement.
Reflect on Experiences: Consider your past work experiences, noting significant achievements and challenges. What did you learn from these experiences?
Identify Strengths and Weaknesses: Recognize your strengths that can be leveraged for career growth and pinpoint weaknesses that require attention.
Setting Clear and Achievable Goals
Goal setting is a cornerstone of a professional development plan. Your goals should be specific, measurable, achievable, relevant, and time-bound (SMART):

Short-Term Goals: Set goals you aim to achieve within the next 6 to 12 months. These could include completing a certification, improving a particular skill, or taking on a new project at work.

Long-Term Goals: Define your career aspirations for the next 3 to 5 years. This could involve aiming for a promotion, transitioning to a new industry, or gaining leadership experience.

Identifying Career Options

Explore various career paths and opportunities that align with your skills and interests:

Research Industries: Investigate different industries to understand their growth potential, job opportunities, and required skills.

Network with Professionals: Connect with individuals in your desired field to gain insights and advice. Informational interviews can provide valuable perspectives.

Match Skills and Interests: Consider how your skills and passions align with potential career options. Choose paths that excite you and where you can make a meaningful impact.

Creating a Career Action Plan

Develop a structured action plan that outlines the steps needed to achieve your goals:

Outline Steps: Break down each goal into smaller, manageable tasks. For instance, if your goal is to earn a certification, steps might include researching programs, enrolling in a course, and scheduling study time.

Set Timelines: Assign deadlines to each task to create a sense of urgency and accountability. Ensure these timelines are realistic and achievable.

Track Progress: Regularly monitor your progress towards your goals. Use tools like progress trackers, journals, or digital apps to stay organized and focused.

Adapting to Change

Career planning is not static; it requires flexibility and adaptability:

Stay Open to Opportunities: Be receptive to new opportunities that may arise, even if they weren't part of your original plan. Sometimes unexpected paths lead to significant growth.
Reassess Goals: Periodically review and reassess your goals. Adjust them based on changes in your interests, industry trends, or life circumstances.
Update Skills: Continuously seek opportunities to learn and develop new skills. Stay informed about industry developments and be proactive in acquiring relevant expertise.

Practical Examples

Example 1: Early-Career Professional

Current Position: Marketing assistant with strong skills in social media management but limited experience in data analytics.
Short-Term Goal: Complete an online course in data analytics within six months.
Long-Term Goal: Transition to a data-driven marketing analyst role within three years.
Career Action Plan: Enroll in a reputable data analytics course, schedule weekly study sessions, apply data skills in current role, seek feedback from supervisors, and network with data professionals.

Example 2: Mid-Career Manager

Current Position: Project manager with a track record of successful projects but no formal leadership training.
Short-Term Goal: Attend a leadership workshop within the next year.
Long-Term Goal: Move into a senior management position within five years.

Career Action Plan: Research leadership workshops, register for a course, practice leadership skills in current projects, seek mentorship from senior leaders, and take on additional leadership responsibilities.

Example 3: Career Changer

Current Position: Teacher looking to transition into corporate training and development.

Short-Term Goal: Obtain a certification in corporate training within the next year.

Long-Term Goal: Secure a corporate training position within two years.

Career Action Plan: Research certification programs, enroll and complete certification, update resume to highlight transferable skills, network with corporate trainers, and apply for relevant positions.

Conclusion

Creating a personalized professional development plan is essential for achieving your career aspirations. By assessing your current position, setting clear and achievable goals, exploring career options, developing a structured action plan, and remaining adaptable to change, you can navigate your career path with confidence and purpose. This proactive approach ensures that you are continually advancing towards your professional objectives, setting yourself up for long-term success and fulfillment.

Chapter 7: The Inner Work - Self-Improvement and Building Self-Confidence

Self-improvement and building self-confidence are fundamental aspects of personal and professional growth. This chapter explores strategies for enhancing your inner self, overcoming obstacles like self-doubt and impostor syndrome, and developing the confidence needed to thrive in your career.

Embracing Self-Improvement
Continuous self-improvement involves a commitment to enhancing your skills, knowledge, and personal attributes. Here are some key strategies:

1. Self-Reflection:

Identify Strengths and Weaknesses: Regularly assess your strengths and areas for improvement. Understanding your capabilities and limitations is the first step towards personal growth.
Set Personal Goals: Establish specific, measurable, achievable, relevant, and time-bound (SMART) goals for self-improvement. This could include learning new skills, developing better habits, or enhancing your emotional intelligence.

Create a Development Plan: Outline a plan that includes the resources, actions, and timelines needed to achieve your personal goals. Regularly review and adjust your plan as you make progress.

2. Seeking Feedback:

Solicit Constructive Criticism: Ask for feedback from colleagues, supervisors, and mentors to gain insights into your performance and areas for improvement.

Reflect on Feedback: Use feedback as a tool for growth. Reflect on the constructive criticism and take actionable steps to address any identified areas for development.

3. Lifelong Learning:

Engage in Continuous Learning: Stay curious and committed to learning throughout your career. Read books, attend workshops, and participate in online courses to expand your knowledge and skills.

Stay Updated: Keep abreast of industry trends, new technologies, and best practices. This ensures that you remain relevant and competitive in your field.

Building Self-Confidence

Self-confidence is the belief in your abilities and judgment. Building self-confidence requires a combination of mindset shifts and practical actions:

1. Positive Self-Talk:

Challenge Negative Thoughts: Identify and counteract negative thoughts that undermine your confidence. Replace them with positive affirmations and constructive self-talk.

Celebrate Successes: Acknowledge and celebrate your achievements, no matter how small. Recognizing your accomplishments helps build a positive self-image.

2. Setting Achievable Goals:

Start Small: Set small, achievable goals that allow you to experience success and build confidence gradually. As you accomplish these goals, set progressively larger ones.
Track Progress: Keep a record of your achievements and progress. This visual reminder of your growth can boost your confidence.
3. Facing Challenges:

Step Out of Your Comfort Zone: Regularly challenge yourself to take on tasks or projects that push your boundaries. Facing and overcoming challenges builds resilience and confidence.
Learn from Failure: View failures as learning opportunities rather than setbacks. Analyze what went wrong, identify lessons learned, and apply them to future endeavors.
Overcoming Self-Doubt and Impostor Syndrome
Self-doubt and impostor syndrome can hinder your confidence and professional growth. Here's how to overcome these challenges:

1. Recognize Self-Doubt:

Acknowledge Your Feelings: Understand that self-doubt is a common experience. Recognize when you are feeling doubtful and identify the triggers.
Seek Support: Talk to trusted colleagues, mentors, or friends about your feelings. Often, discussing your doubts can provide reassurance and perspective.
2. Addressing Impostor Syndrome:

Acknowledge Achievements: Keep a record of your successes and positive feedback. Reviewing these can help counteract feelings of inadequacy.
Reframe Your Thoughts: Challenge the belief that you are a fraud. Remind yourself that your achievements are the result of your hard work and capabilities.

Seek Validation: Don't hesitate to ask for feedback on your performance. Constructive validation from others can reinforce your self-worth.

Practical Examples and Case Studies

Example 1: Overcoming Self-Doubt

Jane, a marketing executive, often feels overwhelmed by new projects. By setting small, manageable goals and seeking feedback from her mentor, she gradually builds confidence in her abilities. Celebrating each milestone helps her see her progress, reducing her self-doubt.

Example 2: Facing Challenges

Tom, a software developer, decides to lead a complex project for the first time. Initially anxious, he steps out of his comfort zone, seeks guidance from experienced colleagues, and learns from minor setbacks. Successfully completing the project significantly boosts his confidence.

Example 3: Battling Impostor Syndrome

Sara, a newly promoted manager, feels like she doesn't deserve her position. She keeps a journal of her achievements and positive feedback, which she reviews whenever she feels inadequate. Discussing her feelings with a mentor helps her see her true worth.

Actionable Tips for Implementation

1. Practice Self-Reflection:

Dedicate time each week for self-reflection. Consider what went well, what didn't, and how you can improve.

2. Seek Feedback Regularly:

Set up regular feedback sessions with your supervisor or mentor to gain insights into your performance.

3. Engage in Learning Activities:

Allocate time for professional development activities, such as reading industry-related articles, attending webinars, or taking online courses.

4. Build a Support Network:

Surround yourself with supportive colleagues and mentors who encourage your growth and provide constructive feedback.

5. Embrace Challenges:

Take on new tasks and projects that push you out of your comfort zone, even if they seem daunting at first.

By focusing on self-improvement and building self-confidence, you can overcome personal obstacles, achieve professional growth, and enhance your overall career satisfaction. This inner work is crucial for long-term success and fulfillment in your chosen field.

Chapter 8: Strategies for Personal Growth and Self-Improvement

Personal growth and self-improvement are ongoing processes that are vital for achieving long-term success and fulfillment in your career. This chapter outlines practical strategies to help you continually develop your skills, enhance your abilities, and reach your full potential.

Embracing a Growth Mindset
A growth mindset is the belief that abilities and intelligence can be developed through dedication and hard work. This mindset is crucial for personal growth and self-improvement:

Adopt Positive Thinking: Cultivate an attitude of positivity and possibility. View challenges as opportunities to learn rather than as obstacles.
Embrace Learning: Commit to lifelong learning and see every experience as a chance to gain new knowledge and skills.
Accept Feedback: Be open to constructive criticism. Use feedback as a tool for improvement rather than taking it personally.
Setting SMART Goals
Setting goals that are specific, measurable, achievable, relevant, and time-bound (SMART) is essential for personal growth:

Specific: Clearly define what you want to achieve. For example, instead of saying "I want to improve my public speaking," specify "I want to give a confident presentation at the next team meeting."

Measurable: Ensure your goal has criteria for measuring progress. This could be the number of presentations given or the amount of positive feedback received.

Achievable: Set realistic goals that are within your capacity to achieve, considering your current skills and resources.

Relevant: Align your goals with your broader career aspirations. Make sure they contribute to your overall personal and professional development.

Time-Bound: Set a deadline for achieving your goals. This helps create a sense of urgency and keeps you focused.

Continuous Learning and Skill Development

Staying updated with industry trends and acquiring new skills are key components of personal growth:

Formal Education: Consider enrolling in degree programs, certifications, or specialized courses that advance your career.

Informal Learning: Engage in self-study by reading books, listening to podcasts, and following industry blogs. Online platforms like Coursera, edX, and Udemy offer valuable resources.

Workshops and Seminars: Attend industry workshops, seminars, and conferences to learn from experts and network with peers.

Building Self-Awareness

Understanding your strengths, weaknesses, values, and motivations is essential for personal growth:

Reflect Regularly: Take time to reflect on your experiences, what you've learned, and how you can improve. Journaling can be a useful tool for self-reflection.

Seek Feedback: Regularly ask for feedback from colleagues, mentors, and supervisors to gain different perspectives on your performance and areas for growth.
Assess Your Skills: Use self-assessment tools and personality tests to gain deeper insights into your abilities and preferences.

Developing Emotional Intelligence

Emotional intelligence (EI) is the ability to understand and manage your emotions and the emotions of others. It plays a critical role in personal and professional relationships:

Self-Awareness: Recognize your own emotions and how they affect your thoughts and behavior.
Self-Regulation: Develop the ability to control impulsive feelings and behaviors, manage your emotions in healthy ways, and adapt to changing circumstances.
Social Skills: Improve your communication skills, develop strong relationships, and build networks.
Empathy: Understand and share the feelings of others. This helps in building stronger interpersonal connections.

Cultivating Resilience

Resilience is the capacity to recover quickly from difficulties. Building resilience helps you navigate the ups and downs of your career:

Develop a Positive Attitude: Focus on the positive aspects of any situation and learn from setbacks.
Build a Support Network: Surround yourself with supportive colleagues, friends, and family who can offer assistance and encouragement.
Practice Self-Care: Take care of your physical and mental health through regular exercise, a healthy diet, sufficient sleep, and mindfulness practices like meditation.

Engaging in Mentorship and Coaching

Mentorship and coaching can provide valuable guidance and support for personal growth:

Seek Mentors: Find mentors who can offer advice, share experiences, and provide feedback. A mentor can help you navigate career challenges and opportunities.

Participate in Coaching: Engage in professional coaching to gain personalized guidance and support. Coaches can help you set and achieve personal and professional goals.

Mentor Others: Serving as a mentor to others can also enhance your own skills and provide new perspectives.

Practical Examples and Case Studies

Example 1: Adopting a Growth Mindset

Emily, an engineer, faced challenges with a new technology at work. Instead of seeing this as a setback, she adopted a growth mindset, took an online course, and sought help from colleagues. Her proactive approach not only improved her skills but also increased her confidence.

Example 2: Setting SMART Goals

David, a marketing professional, wanted to improve his digital marketing skills. He set a SMART goal to complete a certification in digital marketing within six months, allocating specific hours each week for study. This structured approach helped him successfully achieve his goal.

Example 3: Building Resilience

Alex, a project manager, encountered a major project failure. Instead of being disheartened, he analyzed what went wrong, sought feedback, and focused on learning from the experience. His resilience helped him manage future projects more effectively.

Actionable Tips for Implementation

1. Create a Personal Development Plan:

Outline your SMART goals and the steps needed to achieve them. Regularly review and update your plan as you make progress.

2. Allocate Time for Learning:

Dedicate specific time slots each week for learning activities, whether it's reading, taking courses, or attending seminars.

3. Practice Self-Reflection:

Set aside time at the end of each day or week to reflect on your experiences and identify areas for improvement.

4. Build Your Emotional Intelligence:

Engage in activities that enhance your EI, such as mindfulness meditation, empathy exercises, and effective communication practices.

5. Seek and Act on Feedback:

Regularly ask for feedback from trusted sources and take actionable steps to address the feedback received.

6. Develop Resilience:

Practice self-care, build a strong support network, and maintain a positive outlook to enhance your resilience in the face of challenges.

By implementing these strategies for personal growth and self-improvement, you can continuously enhance your capabilities, overcome obstacles, and achieve greater success in your personal and professional life.

Chapter 9: Developing Self-Confidence in the Workplace

Self-confidence is a critical component of professional success and personal fulfillment. In the workplace, confidence enables you to take on new challenges, communicate effectively, and lead with authority. This chapter explores practical strategies to develop and enhance your self-confidence at work.

Understanding the Importance of Self-Confidence
Self-confidence impacts every aspect of your career, from daily interactions to long-term achievements:

Enhanced Performance: Confident individuals are more likely to perform well under pressure and tackle difficult tasks with a positive attitude.
Effective Communication: Confidence helps you articulate your ideas clearly and persuasively, leading to better collaboration and influence.
Leadership Abilities: Self-assured leaders inspire trust and respect, motivating their teams to achieve common goals.
Career Advancement: Employers value confident employees who can take initiative and drive projects forward, leading to greater opportunities for career growth.
Building Self-Confidence: Practical Strategies
1. Self-Awareness and Self-Acceptance

Understand Your Strengths and Weaknesses: Conduct an honest self-assessment to identify your strengths and areas for improvement. Celebrate your strengths and create a plan to address weaknesses.

Practice Self-Acceptance: Accept yourself as you are and focus on continuous improvement. Recognize that everyone has limitations and that making mistakes is part of the learning process.

2. Setting Achievable Goals

Start Small: Set small, manageable goals to build a track record of success. Achieving these goals can boost your confidence and encourage you to tackle bigger challenges.

Track Progress: Keep a journal or use a digital tool to track your progress towards your goals. Reviewing your accomplishments regularly can reinforce your sense of achievement and confidence.

3. Skill Development

Invest in Learning: Continuously develop your skills through formal education, workshops, and on-the-job training. Being well-prepared and knowledgeable can significantly boost your confidence.

Seek Feedback: Regularly ask for constructive feedback from peers, mentors, and supervisors. Use this feedback to improve and grow, which in turn will increase your confidence in your abilities.

4. Positive Visualization and Affirmations

Visualize Success: Spend a few minutes each day visualizing yourself succeeding in various tasks and situations. This mental practice can help you approach real-life challenges with a positive mindset.

Use Affirmations: Develop a set of positive affirmations that reinforce your strengths and capabilities. Repeat these affirmations daily to build a positive self-image.

5. Effective Communication Skills

Practice Public Speaking: Join a public speaking group, such as Toastmasters, to practice and improve your speaking skills. Confidence in public speaking can translate to better overall communication.

Active Listening: Improve your listening skills to better understand and respond to colleagues and clients. Effective communication is a two-way street, and being a good listener builds confidence in your interactions.

6. Physical Presence and Body Language

Maintain Good Posture: Stand and sit with good posture to project confidence and authority. Your body language can influence how others perceive you and how you feel about yourself.

Make Eye Contact: Making eye contact during conversations demonstrates confidence and helps build trust with others.

7. Overcoming Self-Doubt and Impostor Syndrome

Acknowledge Self-Doubt: Recognize and acknowledge feelings of self-doubt without letting them control your actions. Understand that many successful people experience these feelings.

Focus on Evidence: Counteract impostor syndrome by focusing on factual evidence of your accomplishments and competencies. Keep a record of positive feedback and achievements to remind yourself of your capabilities.

Practical Examples and Case Studies

Example 1: Gradual Goal Achievement

Linda, a junior analyst, felt overwhelmed by the expectations in her new role. She started by setting small goals, such as mastering specific software tools. Each success boosted her confidence, enabling her to tackle more complex tasks.

Example 2: Public Speaking Confidence

John, a marketing manager, was anxious about presenting at team meetings. He joined a public speaking group and practiced regularly. Over time, his public speaking skills improved, and his confidence grew, positively impacting his performance at work.

Example 3: Overcoming Impostor Syndrome
Rachel, a newly promoted team leader, struggled with feelings of inadequacy. She began documenting her achievements and regularly sought feedback from her mentor. This helped her see her true value and capabilities, reducing her impostor syndrome.

Actionable Tips for Implementation
1. Develop a Personal Confidence Plan:

Create a plan that includes specific actions to build your confidence, such as setting achievable goals, seeking feedback, and practicing new skills.
2. Engage in Continuous Learning:

Dedicate time each week to learning and professional development activities. This could include taking online courses, reading industry-related materials, or attending workshops.
3. Practice Positive Visualization:

Spend a few minutes each day visualizing successful outcomes in your tasks and interactions. This can help you approach real-life situations with a positive mindset.
4. Join Supportive Communities:

Join professional groups or communities, such as public speaking clubs or industry associations, where you can practice skills and gain support from peers.
5. Keep a Confidence Journal:

Maintain a journal where you document your successes, positive feedback, and moments when you felt confident. Reviewing this journal can boost your self-esteem and remind you of your capabilities.

By implementing these strategies, you can develop and enhance your self-confidence in the workplace. Confidence is not just an innate trait but a skill that can be nurtured and developed over time. With increased self-assurance, you'll be better equipped to face challenges, seize opportunities, and achieve your professional goals.

Chapter 10: Overcoming Self-Doubt and Impostor Syndrome

Self-doubt and impostor syndrome are common challenges that can hinder professional growth and personal fulfillment. This chapter delves into understanding these issues and provides practical strategies to overcome them, empowering you to achieve your full potential with confidence.

Understanding Self-Doubt and Impostor Syndrome
Self-Doubt:
Self-doubt involves questioning your abilities, decisions, and worth. It can manifest as hesitation, fear of failure, and reluctance to take on new challenges.

Impostor Syndrome:
Impostor syndrome is a psychological pattern where individuals doubt their accomplishments and fear being exposed as a "fraud." Despite evidence of their competence, those experiencing impostor syndrome feel unworthy of their success.

Recognizing the Signs
Perfectionism: Setting excessively high standards and feeling like a failure if you don't meet them.
Attributing Success to Luck: Believing that your achievements are due to luck or external factors rather than your skills and efforts.

Fear of Failure: Avoiding new challenges or opportunities due to fear of not being good enough.

Undermining Achievements: Downplaying your accomplishments and feeling like you don't deserve recognition.

Strategies for Overcoming Self-Doubt and Impostor Syndrome

1. Acknowledge and Understand Your Feelings

Accept Self-Doubt: Recognize that self-doubt is a natural part of growth. Everyone experiences it at some point in their career.

Identify Triggers: Understand the situations or tasks that trigger self-doubt and impostor feelings. Awareness is the first step to overcoming them.

2. Reframe Negative Thoughts

Challenge Negative Beliefs: When you catch yourself thinking negatively, ask if there's evidence to support those thoughts. Replace them with positive, factual statements about your abilities.

Practice Self-Compassion: Treat yourself with the same kindness and understanding that you would offer to a friend in a similar situation.

3. Celebrate Your Successes

Keep an Achievement Journal: Document your accomplishments, positive feedback, and instances where you overcame challenges. Reviewing this regularly can reinforce your self-worth.

Acknowledge Milestones: Celebrate your progress and achievements, no matter how small. This helps build a positive self-image.

4. Seek Support and Mentorship

Talk About Your Feelings: Share your experiences with trusted friends, colleagues, or mentors. They can provide perspective and reassurance.

Find a Mentor: A mentor can offer guidance, share their own experiences with self-doubt, and help you navigate your career path with more confidence.

5. Focus on Continuous Learning

Invest in Your Skills: Continuously improve your skills through training, courses, and professional development. The more knowledgeable and skilled you become, the more confident you will feel.

Embrace a Growth Mindset: View challenges and failures as opportunities to learn and grow rather than as reflections of your inadequacy.

6. Take Action Despite Self-Doubt

Step Out of Your Comfort Zone: Regularly take on tasks that challenge you. Each successful experience will build your confidence and reduce self-doubt.

Set Realistic Goals: Break down larger goals into smaller, manageable tasks. Achieving these smaller tasks can provide a sense of accomplishment and motivation.

7. Practice Mindfulness and Stress Management

Mindfulness Techniques: Practices like meditation and deep breathing can help reduce anxiety and increase self-awareness.

Healthy Lifestyle: Maintain a balanced diet, regular exercise, and adequate sleep to support your overall well-being and mental health.

Practical Examples and Case Studies

Example 1: Reframing Negative Thoughts

Sarah, a project manager, often felt she wasn't competent enough for her role. She started a practice of writing down her negative thoughts and then writing a positive counter-statement. Over time, she began to see her true value and contributions to the team.

Example 2: Celebrating Successes
James, a junior lawyer, kept a journal of his successful cases and positive feedback from clients. Reviewing his achievements helped him combat feelings of inadequacy and boosted his confidence in his legal skills.

Example 3: Seeking Mentorship
Linda, a software engineer, felt out of place in her new senior role. She reached out to a mentor in the tech industry who shared similar experiences. This mentorship provided Linda with valuable advice and reassurance, helping her navigate her new responsibilities with confidence.

Actionable Tips for Implementation
1. Create a Positive Affirmation Routine:

Start your day with positive affirmations that reinforce your strengths and capabilities. For example, "I am competent and capable in my role."
2. Maintain a Success Log:

Regularly update a log of your achievements, positive feedback, and any successful outcomes. Review this log whenever you feel self-doubt creeping in.
3. Develop a Support Network:

Surround yourself with supportive colleagues, friends, and mentors who can offer encouragement and constructive feedback.
4. Commit to Lifelong Learning:

Allocate time each week for learning new skills or enhancing existing ones. This commitment to growth will help reinforce your self-confidence.

5. Practice Mindfulness:

Incorporate mindfulness practices into your daily routine to help manage stress and maintain a positive mindset.

By understanding and addressing self-doubt and impostor syndrome, you can build a stronger, more confident professional identity. These strategies will help you navigate challenges, seize opportunities, and achieve greater success and fulfillment in your career.

Chapter 11: The Job Hunt - Navigating the Job Search

Navigating the job search process can be both exciting and daunting. This chapter provides a comprehensive guide to help you effectively navigate the job market, from preparing for your job search to securing your desired position.

Understanding the Job Market Landscape
1. Assessing Your Career Goals and Preferences

Self-Assessment: Reflect on your skills, strengths, and career aspirations. Identify industries and roles that align with your interests and goals.
Research: Conduct research on companies and industries of interest. Understand their values, culture, and growth opportunities.
2. Crafting a Compelling Resume and Cover Letter

Resume Essentials: Create a targeted resume that highlights your relevant skills, experiences, and achievements. Tailor your resume to each job application to showcase your fit for the role.

Effective Cover Letters: Write customized cover letters that demonstrate your enthusiasm for the position and how your skills align with the company's needs.

3. Utilizing Online Platforms and Networking

Online Job Boards: Utilize job search engines and company websites to find job openings. Set up job alerts to stay informed about new opportunities.

Networking Strategies: Build and leverage your professional network through platforms like LinkedIn, industry events, and informational interviews. Networking can uncover hidden job opportunities and provide valuable referrals.

4. Effective Job Search Strategies

Targeted Applications: Focus on quality over quantity when applying for jobs. Tailor your application materials to match the job description and company culture.

Follow-Up: After submitting an application, follow up with a polite email or phone call to express your continued interest in the position.

5. Preparing for Different Types of Interviews

Interview Preparation: Research the company, review common interview questions, and practice your responses. Prepare examples that showcase your skills and accomplishments.

Virtual Interviews: Familiarize yourself with virtual interview platforms and ensure a professional setting with good lighting and minimal distractions.

6. Negotiating Salary and Benefits

Salary Research: Research industry standards and salary ranges for your position and location. Prepare to negotiate based on your skills, experience, and the company's compensation package.

Benefits Consideration: Evaluate the overall compensation package, including benefits such as healthcare, retirement plans, and professional development opportunities.

Practical Examples and Case Studies

Example 1: Effective Networking

Jack, a marketing professional, attended industry conferences and connected with peers and leaders in his field. Through networking, he learned about an unadvertised job opening and secured an interview, ultimately landing the job.

Example 2: Tailored Applications

Sarah, a software developer, customized her resume and cover letter for each job application, highlighting her relevant skills and experiences. This targeted approach helped her stand out to employers and secure multiple interview opportunities.

Example 3: Successful Salary Negotiation

Tom, a project manager, researched salary benchmarks for his role and location. During negotiations, he confidently presented his achievements and skills, leading to a higher salary offer and additional benefits.

Actionable Tips for Implementation

1. Develop a Job Search Plan:

Set clear goals and timelines for your job search. Allocate time each day or week for researching opportunities, networking, and applying for jobs.

2. Customize Your Application Materials:

Tailor your resume and cover letter to each job application. Highlight relevant skills and experiences that match the job requirements and company culture.

3. Build and Leverage Your Network:

Connect with professionals in your industry through networking events, LinkedIn, and informational interviews. Nurture these relationships for ongoing career growth.

4. Practice Interview Skills:

Prepare thoroughly for interviews by researching the company, practicing responses to common interview questions, and conducting mock interviews with friends or mentors.

5. Negotiate Confidently:

Research salary ranges and benefits before negotiations. Practice articulating your value and be prepared to discuss compensation and benefits in a professional manner.

By implementing these strategies, you can navigate the job search process effectively and increase your chances of securing a position that aligns with your career goals and aspirations. Stay proactive, persistent, and adaptable throughout your job search journey to achieve success.

Chapter 12: Effective Job Search Strategies in a Digital Age

In today's digital landscape, the job search process has evolved significantly. This chapter explores practical strategies and tools to help you navigate the digital job market successfully, leveraging technology to enhance your job search efforts.

Embracing Online Platforms and Resources
1. Utilizing Job Search Engines and Websites

Job Search Engines: Use platforms like Indeed, Glassdoor, and LinkedIn to search for job openings across various industries and locations.
Company Websites: Visit company career pages directly to explore job opportunities and learn more about their organizational culture and values.
2. Building a Strong Online Presence

Optimize Your LinkedIn Profile: Create a professional LinkedIn profile that highlights your skills, experiences, and career accomplishments. Connect with industry professionals and join relevant groups.

Personal Website or Portfolio: Showcase your work, projects, and achievements on a personal website or portfolio to demonstrate your skills and expertise to potential employers.

3. Networking in the Digital Era

LinkedIn Networking: Engage with industry professionals, recruiters, and potential employers on LinkedIn. Share industry insights, participate in discussions, and build meaningful connections.

Virtual Networking Events: Attend virtual networking events, webinars, and online conferences to expand your professional network and discover new job opportunities.

Crafting a Compelling Digital Resume and Cover Letter

1. Tailoring Your Resume for ATS

Keyword Optimization: Customize your resume with relevant keywords from job descriptions to increase visibility to Applicant Tracking Systems (ATS).

Formatting: Use a clean, professional format with bullet points to highlight key achievements and skills quickly.

2. Writing Effective Cover Letters

Customization: Personalize each cover letter to address specific job requirements and company needs. Express your enthusiasm for the position and how your skills align with the role.

Storytelling: Use storytelling techniques to showcase your accomplishments and career journey, demonstrating your fit for the position.

Leveraging Technology for Job Search Efficiency

1. Setting Up Job Alerts

Email Notifications: Subscribe to job alerts on job search platforms to receive email notifications for new job postings matching your criteria.

Mobile Apps: Use mobile apps for job search platforms to stay updated on the go and apply for jobs conveniently.

2. Virtual Interviews and Assessments

Preparing for Virtual Interviews: Familiarize yourself with video conferencing tools, test your equipment, and ensure a professional background and appearance.

Online Assessments: Be prepared for online assessments or tests that employers may use to evaluate your skills and qualifications.

Staying Organized and Engaged

1. Creating a Job Search Schedule

Time Management: Allocate dedicated time each day or week for job searching, networking, and application submissions.

Tracking Applications: Keep a record of jobs applied for, application deadlines, and follow-up actions to stay organized and proactive.

2. Engaging with Industry Insights and Trends

Following Industry Leaders: Follow industry influencers, companies, and thought leaders on social media platforms to stay updated on industry trends and developments.

Continuing Education: Take advantage of online courses, webinars, and certifications to enhance your skills and knowledge, making you a more competitive candidate.

Practical Examples and Case Studies

Example 1: Leveraging LinkedIn for Networking

David, a marketing professional, optimized his LinkedIn profile with relevant keywords and regularly shared industry insights and articles. Through proactive networking, he connected with a recruiter who introduced him to a senior role at a leading company.

Example 2: Using Job Search Alerts
Emily, a recent graduate, set up job alerts on multiple job search platforms. She received daily notifications for entry-level positions in her field, allowing her to apply promptly and secure interviews with several companies.

Example 3: Virtual Interview Success
Michael, a software engineer, prepared for a virtual interview by testing his video setup and conducting mock interviews with friends. His confident performance during the interview impressed the hiring manager, leading to a job offer.

Actionable Tips for Implementation
1. Update Your Online Presence Regularly:

Maintain an updated LinkedIn profile and personal website/portfolio showcasing your latest achievements and skills.
2. Customize Applications for Each Job:

Tailor your resume and cover letter to align with specific job requirements and company culture, increasing your chances of standing out to employers.
3. Stay Informed About Industry Changes:

Follow industry news, trends, and innovations to demonstrate your industry knowledge and adaptability during interviews and networking interactions.
4. Network Proactively:

Engage with professionals in your field through LinkedIn, attend virtual networking events, and join industry-specific groups to expand your network and uncover hidden job opportunities.

By implementing these strategies, you can effectively navigate the digital job market, enhance your visibility to employers, and secure meaningful career opportunities aligned with your professional goals and aspirations.

Chapter 13: Utilizing Online Platforms and Networking for Job Hunting

In today's digital age, online platforms and networking play pivotal roles in successful job hunting strategies. This chapter explores effective methods for leveraging digital tools and networks to maximize your job search efforts and connect with potential employers.

Harnessing the Power of Online Job Platforms
1. Major Job Search Engines and Websites

Indeed, Glassdoor, LinkedIn: Utilize popular job search engines like Indeed and Glassdoor, as well as professional networking platforms such as LinkedIn, to explore job opportunities across diverse industries.
Company Career Pages: Visit the career pages of companies you are interested in to directly apply for roles and learn about their corporate culture and values.
2. Setting Up Job Alerts and Notifications

Email Alerts: Subscribe to job alerts on various job search platforms to receive notifications about new job openings that match your criteria.

Mobile Apps: Download mobile applications for job search platforms to stay updated on the go and apply for jobs conveniently.

Crafting an Effective Online Presence

1. Optimizing Your LinkedIn Profile

Professional Headline and Summary: Create a compelling headline and summary that highlight your skills, experiences, and career objectives. Use keywords relevant to your industry.

Skills and Endorsements: List your skills and seek endorsements from colleagues and connections to enhance your profile's credibility.

2. Developing a Personal Website or Portfolio

Showcase Your Work: Create a personal website or online portfolio to showcase your projects, achievements, and work samples. This can provide a deeper insight into your skills and abilities beyond your resume.

Blog or Content Sharing: Share industry insights, articles, and professional achievements on your website or blog to demonstrate thought leadership and engage with your audience.

Networking Strategies for Job Seekers

1. Building and Expanding Your Network

LinkedIn Networking: Connect with professionals in your industry, recruiters, and potential employers on LinkedIn. Engage in meaningful conversations, join industry groups, and participate in discussions to expand your network.

Networking Events: Attend virtual networking events, webinars, and conferences related to your field to establish new connections and stay updated on industry trends.

2. Informational Interviews and Referrals

Requesting Informational Interviews: Reach out to professionals in your network for informational interviews to gain insights into their career paths and industry experiences.
Referrals and Recommendations: Leverage your network to seek referrals and recommendations for job opportunities within companies of interest. Personal recommendations can significantly enhance your candidacy.
Leveraging Social Media and Online Communities
1. Engaging on Social Media Platforms

Twitter, Facebook Groups: Follow industry leaders and participate in relevant Twitter chats and Facebook groups to stay informed about industry news and job opportunities.
Professional Associations: Join professional associations and groups related to your field to network with peers, share knowledge, and access exclusive job postings.
2. Participating in Online Forums and Discussions

Reddit, Quora: Engage in discussions on platforms like Reddit and Quora to exchange insights, ask questions, and showcase your expertise in specific areas of interest.
Industry-Specific Forums: Participate in industry-specific forums and online communities to connect with professionals, share best practices, and build your reputation within your industry.
Practical Examples and Case Studies
Example 1: LinkedIn Networking Success
Emily, a marketing professional, optimized her LinkedIn profile with relevant keywords and engaged actively by sharing industry articles and insights. She connected with a senior marketing manager who introduced her to a job opportunity that aligned perfectly with her career goals.

Example 2: Personal Website Showcase

John, a graphic designer, developed a personal website showcasing his portfolio of design projects and client testimonials. His online presence impressed a potential employer who reached out directly for an interview, leading to a job offer.

Example 3: Networking Event Impact
Sarah, a recent graduate in finance, attended a virtual networking event hosted by a professional association. Through networking conversations, she connected with a financial analyst who referred her for an entry-level position at a leading financial institution.

Actionable Tips for Implementation
1. Maintain a Professional Online Presence:

Regularly update your LinkedIn profile with new skills, experiences, and achievements. Share industry-related content to demonstrate your expertise and engage with your network.
2. Expand Your Network Strategically:

Connect with professionals in your field and industry influencers. Personalize connection requests and engage in meaningful conversations to build mutually beneficial relationships.
3. Actively Participate in Online Communities:

Join relevant LinkedIn groups, participate in Twitter chats, and contribute valuable insights on platforms like Reddit and Quora to establish your credibility and expand your professional network.
4. Stay Organized and Persistent:

Keep track of your networking efforts, job applications, and follow-up actions. Set aside dedicated time each day or week for online networking activities and job search activities to stay proactive and organized.

By implementing these strategies and leveraging digital platforms effectively, you can enhance your visibility to employers, expand your professional network, and uncover rewarding job opportunities aligned with your career aspirations.

Chapter 14: Crafting a Compelling Resume and Cover Letter

Your resume and cover letter are essential tools that showcase your qualifications, skills, and experiences to potential employers. This chapter provides expert guidance on creating compelling resume and cover letter documents that capture attention and highlight your suitability for the desired position.

Building Your Professional Resume
1. Structuring Your Resume Effectively

Header: Include your name, contact information, and LinkedIn profile URL at the top of the resume for easy reference.

Professional Summary: Write a concise summary highlighting your key skills, experiences, and career achievements. Tailor this section to align with the job you're applying for.

Skills Section: List relevant technical skills, soft skills, and certifications that are pertinent to the job role and industry.

Work Experience: Detail your work history in reverse chronological order. Include the company name, job title, dates of employment, and key responsibilities and achievements for each role.

Education: Provide details of your educational background, including degrees, certifications, and any relevant coursework or academic achievements.

2. Tailoring Your Resume for Each Application

Keyword Optimization: Customize your resume to include keywords and phrases from the job description. This helps ATS (Applicant Tracking Systems) identify your resume as a match for the position.

Highlight Achievements: Use bullet points to quantify your achievements and demonstrate the impact of your work using metrics and numbers where possible.

Formatting: Ensure your resume is well-organized, easy to read, and visually appealing. Use a clean, professional font and maintain consistent formatting throughout.

Crafting a Persuasive Cover Letter

1. Addressing the Hiring Manager

Personalization: Address the cover letter to the hiring manager or recruiter whenever possible. Research the company to find the name of the appropriate contact person.

Introduction: Start with a strong opening paragraph that expresses your interest in the position and introduces yourself briefly.

Showcasing Your Fit: Highlight specific skills, experiences, and achievements that align with the job requirements and company culture.

Demonstrating Passion: Share why you are enthusiastic about the opportunity and how your skills and goals align with the company's mission and values.

Closing Statement: Conclude with a call to action, expressing your desire for an interview and thanking the reader for their time and consideration.

Enhancing Your Application Package

1. Proofreading and Editing

Review for Errors: Thoroughly proofread your resume and cover letter for spelling, grammar, and formatting errors. Consider asking a trusted friend or mentor to review your documents as well.

Consistency: Ensure consistency in language and formatting between your resume, cover letter, and other application materials.

2. Seeking Feedback

Peer Review: Seek feedback from peers, mentors, or career advisors to ensure your resume and cover letter effectively showcase your strengths and qualifications.

Customization: Tailor each cover letter to reflect your understanding of the company and the specific role you are applying for. Avoid generic templates.

Practical Examples and Case Studies

Example 1: Results-Oriented Resume

Amy, a sales manager, crafted a resume that quantified her achievements with specific sales figures and percentages. Her results-oriented approach demonstrated her impact and contributions to previous employers, attracting the attention of hiring managers.

Example 2: Personalized Cover Letter

John, a software developer, researched the company's culture and recent projects. His cover letter highlighted his technical skills and experience in developing software solutions aligned with the company's current needs, resulting in an interview invitation.

Example 3: Effective Application Package
Sarah, a marketing specialist, consistently tailored her resume and cover letter for each job application. Her attention to detail and alignment with job requirements increased her chances of receiving interview invitations from multiple companies.

Actionable Tips for Implementation
1. Research and Customize:

Research the company and job role thoroughly before crafting your resume and cover letter. Tailor your application materials to align with the company's values, goals, and job requirements.
2. Highlight Achievements:

Use quantifiable metrics and specific examples to showcase your achievements and impact in previous roles. Demonstrate how you can bring value to the prospective employer.
3. Professional Presentation:

Ensure your resume is well-organized, visually appealing, and free of errors. Use a professional font and maintain consistent formatting throughout your documents.
4. Follow-Up Responsibly:

After submitting your application, follow up politely within a reasonable timeframe. Express your continued interest in the position and inquire about the next steps in the hiring process. By applying these strategies and crafting a compelling resume and cover letter tailored to each job application, you can effectively capture the attention of hiring managers, demonstrate your qualifications, and increase your chances of securing interviews and advancing in your career journey.

Chapter 15: Defining Your Path - Setting Career Goals

Setting clear and achievable career goals is essential for professional growth and success. This chapter delves into the process of identifying and defining career goals that align with your aspirations, skills, and values, providing a roadmap for long-term career satisfaction and fulfillment.

Importance of Setting Clear Career Goals
1. Establishing Direction and Focus

Clarity: Define specific career goals that provide a clear direction for your professional development. This helps you prioritize tasks and make informed decisions aligned with your aspirations.
Motivation: Having well-defined goals enhances motivation and commitment to achieving success in your chosen career path.
2. Guiding Professional Development

Skill Enhancement: Identify skills and competencies required to achieve your career goals. Plan for continuous learning and development to acquire necessary skills and stay competitive in your field.

Progress Tracking: Set milestones and timelines to track your progress towards achieving your career objectives. Regularly evaluate and adjust your goals as you gain experience and insights.

Strategies for Setting Effective Career Goals

1. SMART Goal Framework

Specific: Clearly define your goals with specific objectives and outcomes. For example, "Achieve a leadership role in marketing within the next three years."

Measurable: Establish criteria to measure your progress and success. This could include metrics such as sales targets, certifications earned, or projects completed.

Achievable: Set goals that are challenging yet attainable with dedication and effort. Consider your current skills, resources, and opportunities for growth.

Relevant: Ensure your goals align with your values, interests, and long-term career aspirations. Focus on goals that contribute to your overall professional fulfillment.

Time-Bound: Set realistic deadlines to achieve each goal. This provides a sense of urgency and helps you prioritize tasks effectively.

2. Long-Term and Short-Term Goals

Long-Term Goals: Define your ultimate career objectives, such as reaching a specific job title or transitioning into a new industry. Break down long-term goals into manageable steps.

Short-Term Goals: Identify immediate objectives that support your long-term aspirations. These could include acquiring new skills, gaining relevant experience, or completing professional certifications.

Aligning Personal and Professional Aspirations

1. Reflection and Self-Assessment

Values and Interests: Consider your personal values, interests, and passions when setting career goals. Aligning your professional aspirations with your personal values enhances job satisfaction and overall happiness.

Work-Life Balance: Evaluate how your career goals impact your personal life and well-being. Strive for a balance that supports both professional success and personal fulfillment.

2. Seeking Mentorship and Guidance

Career Mentors: Engage with mentors or career coaches who can provide guidance and advice based on their experiences. Seek feedback on your career goals and strategies for achieving them.

Peer Support: Connect with peers and colleagues who share similar career interests. Share insights, challenges, and successes to gain different perspectives and mutual support.

Practical Examples and Case Studies

Example 1: Advancing Career in Technology

Sarah, an IT professional, set a SMART goal to earn a specialized certification within six months. She identified training resources, studied diligently, and achieved her certification, positioning herself for a promotion to a senior role in her company.

Example 2: Transitioning to a New Industry

John, a marketing specialist, developed a short-term goal to network with professionals in the renewable energy sector. Through informational interviews and industry events, he gained insights and connections that facilitated his successful transition to a marketing role in a clean energy startup.

Example 3: Achieving Leadership Excellence

Emily, a project manager, established a long-term goal to become a certified project management professional (PMP) within two years. She enrolled in a PMP preparation course, studied rigorously, and passed the exam, advancing her career prospects and earning recognition for her leadership skills.

Actionable Tips for Implementation
1. Write Down Your Goals:

Document your career goals in a journal or digital planner. Review and revise them regularly to stay focused and motivated.
2. Break Goals into Actionable Steps:

Create a roadmap with specific actions and deadlines for achieving each goal. Prioritize tasks based on their importance and alignment with your career objectives.
3. Stay Flexible and Adapt:

Remain open to unexpected opportunities and changes in your career path. Adjust your goals as needed to accommodate new insights or developments.
4. Celebrate Milestones:

Recognize and celebrate achievements along the way, whether small or significant. Acknowledging milestones boosts morale and reinforces your commitment to professional growth.
By setting clear and achievable career goals, you empower yourself to proactively shape your professional future, enhance your skills and capabilities, and create meaningful opportunities for career advancement and personal fulfillment.

Chapter 16: Importance of Setting Clear, Achievable Career Goals

Setting clear and achievable career goals is not just beneficial but crucial for navigating a successful career path. This chapter explores why defining specific objectives is essential for professional growth and how it empowers individuals to achieve long-term success.

Understanding the Significance of Clear Career Goals
1. Establishing Direction and Focus

Clarity and Purpose: Clear career goals provide a roadmap that guides your professional journey. They help you stay focused on what you want to achieve, ensuring that every action you take aligns with your overarching objectives.

Prioritization: By knowing your goals, you can prioritize tasks and opportunities that contribute directly to your career advancement. This prevents distractions and enhances productivity.

2. Enhancing Motivation and Commitment

Motivational Drive: Having specific career goals fuels your motivation to strive for success. It gives you a sense of purpose and direction, making it easier to overcome challenges and setbacks along the way.

Long-Term Vision: Clear goals inspire long-term commitment to personal and professional development. They encourage continuous learning, skill enhancement, and perseverance in pursuing your aspirations.

Benefits of Achievable Career Goals

1. Measurable Progress and Accountability

Tracking Success: Setting achievable goals allows you to measure your progress effectively. You can break down larger objectives into smaller milestones, celebrating achievements and adjusting strategies as needed.

Accountability: Clear goals provide a benchmark against which you can evaluate your performance. They hold you accountable for your actions, fostering a proactive mindset and personal accountability.

2. Career Advancement and Professional Growth

Opportunity Recognition: Defined goals help you recognize and seize opportunities that align with your career aspirations. They enable you to make informed decisions about job opportunities, skill development, and networking engagements.

Skill Development: Pursuing achievable goals encourages ongoing skill development and competency enhancement. It equips you with the capabilities needed to excel in your current role and prepare for future career progression.

Strategies for Setting and Achieving Clear Career Goals

1. SMART Goal Framework

Specific: Clearly define your goals in terms of what you want to achieve and why it is important. For example, "Earn a certification in digital marketing within the next year."
Measurable: Establish criteria for measuring progress and success, such as completing courses or achieving specific performance metrics.
Achievable: Set goals that are challenging yet realistic based on your current skills, resources, and opportunities for growth.
Relevant: Ensure your goals align with your long-term career aspirations and personal values. Focus on objectives that contribute meaningfully to your professional development.
Time-Bound: Set deadlines for achieving each goal, creating a sense of urgency and providing a timeline for action and accomplishment.

2. Regular Review and Adjustment

Evaluation: Regularly review your career goals to assess progress and adjust strategies as necessary. Reflect on achievements, setbacks, and new insights gained along the way.
Flexibility: Remain adaptable to changes in your career path and external factors. Modify goals to accommodate evolving priorities, opportunities, and personal circumstances.

Practical Examples and Case Studies

Example 1: Career Advancement

John, a software developer, set a goal to lead a project team within two years. He pursued additional training in project management, demonstrated leadership skills in cross-functional projects, and achieved his goal by securing a leadership role in his company.

Example 2: Skill Enhancement

Sarah, a marketing manager, aimed to become proficient in data analytics to enhance her marketing strategies. She enrolled in online courses, applied new skills to analyze campaign performance, and successfully integrated data-driven insights into her marketing plans.

Example 3: Career Transition

Emily, a financial analyst, set a goal to transition from finance to sustainable investing. She networked with professionals in the field, completed relevant certifications, and secured a position in a firm specializing in socially responsible investments.

Actionable Tips for Implementation

1. Write Down Your Goals:

Document your career goals in a journal or digital format. Clearly articulate each goal, including specific objectives, timelines, and reasons for pursuing them.

2. Seek Feedback and Support:

Share your goals with mentors, colleagues, or career advisors. Seek their feedback, guidance, and support in developing actionable strategies for goal achievement.

3. Stay Committed and Resilient:

Maintain a positive mindset and resilience in pursuing your goals. Embrace challenges as opportunities for growth and learning, staying focused on long-term success.

4. Celebrate Achievements:

Acknowledge milestones and achievements along the way. Celebrate your progress to stay motivated and reinforce your commitment to professional growth.

By setting clear and achievable career goals, you empower yourself to proactively shape your professional trajectory, enhance your skills and capabilities, and create meaningful opportunities for advancement and fulfillment in your chosen career path.

Chapter 17: Aligning Personal and Professional Aspirations

Aligning personal aspirations with professional goals is essential for achieving fulfillment and success in your career. This chapter explores strategies to harmonize personal values, interests, and long-term ambitions with professional objectives, ensuring a balanced and purposeful approach to career development.

Understanding Personal Aspirations
1. Identifying Personal Values and Interests

Self-Reflection: Begin by reflecting on your core values, passions, and interests outside of work. Consider what activities bring you joy and fulfillment in your personal life.

Long-Term Vision: Envision where you see yourself in the future, both personally and professionally. Identify overarching goals that resonate with your values and contribute to your overall happiness.

2. Evaluating Career Goals

Career Alignment: Assess how your current career path aligns with your personal aspirations. Determine if your professional goals reflect your values and long-term vision for personal growth.

Adjusting Priorities: Prioritize career objectives that complement your personal aspirations, fostering a sense of purpose and alignment in your daily work.

Strategies for Alignment

1. Setting Holistic Goals

Balancing Priorities: Define career goals that support both professional advancement and personal well-being. Consider how achieving these goals will contribute to a fulfilling life overall.

Integration: Seek opportunities to integrate personal interests into your professional life. This may involve pursuing projects or roles that align with your hobbies or values.

2. Creating a Personal Development Plan

Incorporating Growth Areas: Include personal development goals alongside professional milestones in your plan. Allocate time for activities that enhance both your career skills and personal interests.

SMART Goals: Use the SMART criteria (Specific, Measurable, Achievable, Relevant, Time-bound) to structure goals effectively. This ensures clarity and accountability in pursuing your aspirations.

Balancing Work-Life Integration

1. Establishing Boundaries

Work-Life Harmony: Set boundaries to maintain a healthy balance between work commitments and personal life. Allocate time for family, hobbies, and self-care to prevent burnout and sustain motivation.

Flexible Approaches: Explore flexible work arrangements or remote options that support your personal priorities while fulfilling professional responsibilities.

Practical Examples and Case Studies

Example 1: Career Satisfaction Through Alignment

John, a software engineer, discovered a passion for environmental conservation outside of work. He aligned his career goals with his personal values by transitioning to a tech company specializing in sustainable technologies. This career shift allowed him to merge his professional expertise with his passion for environmental stewardship, enhancing job satisfaction and personal fulfillment.

Example 2: Entrepreneurship and Personal Fulfillment

Sarah, a marketing professional, aspired to launch a social enterprise that addressed community health issues. She aligned her career path by gaining industry experience in healthcare marketing and networking with like-minded professionals. Eventually, Sarah successfully launched her startup, integrating her personal values into her entrepreneurial venture.

Actionable Tips for Implementation

1. Regular Self-Assessment

Reflection: Schedule regular self-assessment sessions to evaluate alignment between your personal aspirations and career goals. Adjust objectives as needed to maintain harmony and fulfillment.

2. Seek Mentorship and Support

Guidance: Engage with mentors or career advisors who can provide insights into balancing personal and professional aspirations. Seek advice on navigating career decisions that align with your values and goals.

3. Foster a Supportive Environment

Network: Build a supportive network of peers and colleagues who share similar values and aspirations. Collaborate on projects or initiatives that promote personal growth and professional development.

By aligning personal aspirations with professional goals, you cultivate a sense of purpose and fulfillment in your career journey. This strategic approach not only enhances job satisfaction but also promotes holistic growth and well-being, ensuring sustained motivation and success in achieving both personal and professional milestones.

Chapter 18: Making Your Mark - Personal Branding

Personal branding is a powerful tool in today's competitive professional landscape. This chapter explores the concept of personal branding, its significance, and strategies to cultivate a strong and authentic personal brand that resonates with your professional goals.

Understanding Personal Branding
1. Definition and Purpose

Personal Identity: Personal branding is the process of defining and managing your professional reputation. It encompasses how others perceive you, your unique strengths, values, and the impression you leave in professional interactions.
Differentiation: A strong personal brand sets you apart from others in your field by highlighting your distinctive skills, expertise, and attributes. It establishes credibility and enhances visibility in your industry.
2. Significance of Personal Branding

Career Advancement: A compelling personal brand positions you as a thought leader and expert in your niche, opening doors to new opportunities, collaborations, and career advancement.

Professional Relationships: It fosters trust and credibility among peers, clients, and employers, facilitating stronger professional relationships and networking opportunities.
Consistency and Authenticity: Building an authentic personal brand ensures consistency in how you present yourself across various platforms, reinforcing your professional identity and values.

Strategies for Developing Your Personal Brand

1. Self-Reflection and Assessment

Identify Your Strengths: Conduct a self-assessment to identify your strengths, skills, and unique attributes that contribute to your professional identity.
Define Your Value Proposition: Clarify what sets you apart from others in your field. Articulate your core values, professional goals, and the value you bring to employers or clients.

2. Establishing an Online Presence

Professional Profile: Create a polished and consistent online presence across platforms such as LinkedIn, professional websites, and social media. Optimize your profiles with keywords relevant to your industry.
Content Sharing: Share relevant industry insights, articles, and original content that showcase your expertise and thought leadership. Engage with professional communities and contribute valuable insights to discussions.

3. Networking and Building Relationships

Attend Networking Events: Participate in industry events, conferences, and seminars to expand your professional network. Build genuine relationships with peers, mentors, and industry influencers.
Seek Mentorship: Connect with mentors who can provide guidance and feedback on developing your personal brand and navigating career challenges.

Leveraging Personal Branding for Career Growth

1. Thought Leadership and Visibility

Publishing Content: Write articles, blog posts, or whitepapers on topics relevant to your industry. Establish yourself as a subject matter expert by sharing valuable knowledge and insights.

Speaking Engagements: Seek opportunities to speak at conferences or webinars. Deliver presentations that showcase your expertise and contribute to industry discussions.

2. Monitoring and Managing Your Brand

Feedback and Adaptation: Solicit feedback from peers, mentors, and colleagues to refine and strengthen your personal brand. Monitor your online presence and adjust strategies based on audience engagement and industry trends.

Case Studies and Examples

Example 1: Career Transition and Personal Branding

Emily, a graphic designer, rebranded herself as a visual storyteller specializing in digital marketing. She revamped her portfolio, created a professional website showcasing her projects, and actively engaged with digital marketing communities. This strategic rebranding led to freelance opportunities and collaborations with digital agencies seeking her creative expertise.

Example 2: Executive Leadership and Thought Leadership

John, a seasoned IT executive, cultivated a personal brand as a thought leader in cybersecurity. He authored thought-provoking articles on cybersecurity trends, spoke at industry conferences, and engaged with cybersecurity professionals on LinkedIn. His strong personal brand positioned him as a trusted advisor and contributed to his appointment as a cybersecurity advisor for a multinational corporation.

Actionable Tips for Implementation

1. Develop a Personal Brand Statement:

Craft a concise statement that defines your unique value proposition, professional strengths, and career goals. Use this statement consistently across your professional communications.

2. Curate Your Online Presence:

Regularly update your professional profiles with relevant achievements, skills, and projects. Showcase your expertise through consistent and engaging content sharing.

3. Network with Intention:

Build relationships with professionals who align with your values and career aspirations. Engage in meaningful conversations and offer support to establish rapport and credibility.

By investing in personal branding, you establish a compelling professional identity that resonates with your career goals and values. This strategic approach not only enhances your visibility and credibility but also fosters opportunities for career growth, leadership roles, and meaningful professional relationships.

Chapter 19: Building and Maintaining a Strong Personal Brand

Building and maintaining a strong personal brand is essential for professionals looking to stand out in today's competitive landscape. This chapter delves into the strategies and best practices necessary to establish a compelling personal brand, leverage social media effectively, and cultivate a robust professional network.

Understanding Personal Branding
1. Defining Your Brand Identity

Self-Reflection: Begin by identifying your core values, strengths, and unique qualities that define your professional identity.
Value Proposition: Clarify what sets you apart from others in your field. Define your expertise, passions, and the value you bring to your industry or community.
2. Establishing a Consistent Presence

Online Platforms: Create and optimize professional profiles on platforms like LinkedIn, ensuring consistency in messaging, visuals, and professional accomplishments.

Personal Website: Develop a personal website or portfolio showcasing your skills, achievements, and thought leadership content.

Leveraging Social Media for Brand Visibility

1. Strategic Content Sharing

Content Strategy: Share relevant industry insights, articles, and original content that demonstrate your expertise and interests.

Engagement: Engage with your audience by participating in discussions, responding to comments, and networking with professionals in your field.

2. Building Thought Leadership

Publishing: Write articles or blog posts on platforms like Medium or LinkedIn Pulse to showcase your knowledge and establish yourself as a thought leader.

Networking: Connect with influencers and peers in your industry to expand your reach and build credibility through association.

Cultivating a Professional Network

1. Networking Strategies

Attend Events: Participate in industry conferences, seminars, and networking events to meet new contacts and strengthen existing relationships.

Online Networking: Engage in LinkedIn groups, Twitter chats, and professional forums to connect with like-minded professionals and expand your network.

2. Maintaining Relationships

Follow-Up: After networking events or online interactions, follow up with personalized messages to nurture relationships and stay top-of-mind.

Offer Value: Provide support, advice, or resources to your network to demonstrate your expertise and willingness to contribute.

Case Studies and Examples

Example 1: Social Media Success

Sarah, a marketing consultant, built a strong personal brand by consistently sharing marketing tips and strategies on LinkedIn. Her engagement with industry professionals and thought-provoking content led to speaking invitations at industry events and consulting opportunities with global brands.

Example 2: Networking Excellence

John, a software engineer, leveraged his professional network to secure a leadership role at a tech startup. By attending meetups, contributing to open-source projects, and connecting with industry influencers on Twitter, he built a reputation as a reliable and knowledgeable professional.

Actionable Tips for Implementation

1. Define Your Brand Voice:

Articulate a clear and consistent message that reflects your values, expertise, and career goals across all platforms.

2. Engage Authentically:

Be genuine and authentic in your interactions online and offline. Show empathy, offer insights, and contribute meaningfully to conversations.

3. Continuously Evaluate and Adapt:

Regularly assess the effectiveness of your personal branding efforts. Adjust strategies based on feedback, engagement metrics, and evolving industry trends.

By focusing on building and maintaining a strong personal brand, you enhance your professional reputation, expand your career opportunities, and establish yourself as a respected authority in your field. This proactive approach not only boosts your visibility but also strengthens your network and fosters long-term career success.

Chapter 20: Mastering Communication - Essential Communication Skills

Effective communication is crucial in every aspect of professional and personal life. This chapter delves into essential communication skills, strategies for improving them, and their significance in achieving career success.

Importance of Effective Communication
1. Foundation of Success

Clarity and Understanding: Effective communication ensures that messages are conveyed clearly and understood accurately, fostering productivity and collaboration in teams.
Building Relationships: Strong communication skills help in establishing trust, resolving conflicts, and cultivating positive relationships with colleagues, clients, and stakeholders.
Essential Communication Skills
1. Verbal Communication

Articulation: Expressing thoughts and ideas clearly and concisely, using appropriate language and tone for different audiences.

Active Listening: Paying full attention to others, understanding their perspectives, and responding thoughtfully.

2. Non-Verbal Communication

Body Language: Utilizing gestures, facial expressions, and posture to convey confidence, openness, and engagement.

Eye Contact: Establishing rapport and showing attentiveness during conversations.

Strategies for Enhancing Communication Skills

1. Practice and Feedback

Role-Playing: Engaging in simulated conversations or presentations to refine communication techniques.

Seeking Feedback: Soliciting constructive feedback from peers, mentors, or supervisors to identify areas for improvement.

2. Tailoring Communication

Adapting to Audiences: Adjusting communication style and content based on the knowledge, preferences, and expectations of listeners.

Clarity in Writing: Crafting clear and concise emails, reports, and presentations that convey information effectively.

Communication in Professional Contexts

1. Team Collaboration

Collaborative Discussions: Facilitating productive discussions, encouraging diverse perspectives, and reaching consensus on decisions.

Conflict Resolution: Addressing disagreements respectfully, seeking common ground, and finding mutually beneficial solutions.

2. Leadership Communication

Inspiring and Motivating: Articulating vision, goals, and expectations clearly to inspire and motivate team members.

Feedback and Coaching: Providing constructive feedback and coaching to support professional growth and development.

Case Studies and Examples

Example 1: Effective Team Communication

Sarah, a project manager, improved team collaboration by implementing regular team meetings and using project management tools to streamline communication. Clear expectations and open dialogue among team members led to increased productivity and project success.

Example 2: Leadership Communication

John, a department head, enhanced leadership communication by organizing quarterly town hall meetings to update employees on company initiatives and gather feedback. His transparent communication style built trust and alignment across the organization.

Actionable Tips for Implementation

1. Continuous Learning

Professional Development: Attend workshops, seminars, or online courses focused on communication skills enhancement.
Reading and Research: Stay informed about communication trends, strategies, and best practices in your industry.

2. Self-Awareness and Reflection

Assessing Communication Styles: Reflect on personal communication strengths and areas for improvement to develop a targeted improvement plan.
Seeking Mentorship: Seek guidance from experienced communicators to refine skills and gain insights into effective communication strategies.

By mastering essential communication skills, professionals can enhance their effectiveness, build strong relationships, and advance their careers. Clear and confident communication not only contributes to individual success but also strengthens team dynamics and organizational performance.

Chapter 21: The Role of Effective Communication in Career Success

Effective communication is not just a skill; it's a cornerstone of career success across all industries and roles. This chapter explores how mastering communication can significantly impact your professional growth, relationship-building abilities, and overall success in the workplace.

Importance of Effective Communication
1. Foundation of Professional Relationships

Building Trust: Clear and open communication fosters trust among colleagues, clients, and stakeholders, paving the way for productive collaborations and partnerships.
Conflict Resolution: Effective communication skills enable professionals to navigate conflicts constructively, finding mutually beneficial resolutions.
2. Leadership and Influence

Inspiring Others: Leaders who communicate effectively can articulate visions, goals, and strategies in a compelling manner, inspiring teams to achieve exceptional results.

Influence and Persuasion: Persuasive communication skills empower professionals to influence decisions, gain buy-in from stakeholders, and drive initiatives forward.

Communication Competencies for Career Success

1. Verbal and Non-Verbal Communication

Clarity and Conciseness: Articulating ideas clearly and concisely, ensuring messages are easily understood by diverse audiences.

Non-Verbal Cues: Using body language, facial expressions, and gestures to reinforce verbal messages and convey confidence and credibility.

2. Listening Skills

Active Listening: Paying attention to verbal and non-verbal cues, demonstrating empathy, and showing genuine interest in others' perspectives.

Feedback: Providing constructive feedback and actively seeking input to foster collaborative relationships and continuous improvement.

Communication in Different Professional Contexts

1. Team Collaboration

Effective Meetings: Facilitating productive discussions, ensuring all voices are heard, and summarizing key points to maintain clarity and alignment.

Collaborative Problem-Solving: Engaging team members in brainstorming sessions and guiding discussions toward innovative solutions.

2. Client and Stakeholder Management

Building Rapport: Establishing rapport through effective communication to understand client needs, expectations, and concerns.

Managing Expectations: Setting clear expectations, providing regular updates, and addressing feedback promptly to maintain strong client relationships.

Case Studies and Examples

Example 1: Project Management Success

Sarah, a project manager, demonstrated strong communication skills by effectively coordinating with cross-functional teams, clarifying project goals, and resolving conflicts promptly. Her proactive communication approach contributed to project completion ahead of schedule and within budget.

Example 2: Leadership Excellence

John, a senior executive, exemplified leadership communication by fostering an open-door policy, encouraging transparent communication across departments, and soliciting input from employees at all levels. His approach cultivated a collaborative culture and boosted employee engagement and morale.

Actionable Strategies for Enhancing Communication Skills

1. Continuous Learning and Development

Training and Workshops: Participate in communication skills workshops, seminars, or online courses to enhance verbal, written, and interpersonal communication abilities.

Reading and Research: Stay updated on communication trends, best practices, and industry-specific communication norms to adapt your skills accordingly.

2. Practice and Feedback

Role-Playing Exercises: Engage in role-playing scenarios to practice challenging communication situations and refine responses.

Seeking Mentorship: Seek guidance from mentors or peers who excel in communication to gain insights, feedback, and practical advice for improvement.

By prioritizing effective communication skills, professionals can build meaningful relationships, foster collaborative environments, and achieve career success. Mastering communication not only enhances individual performance but also contributes to organizational effectiveness and growth in today's competitive workplace landscape.

Chapter 22: Techniques and strategies related to active listening and persuasive communication.

Here are some key points that might be discussed in such a chapter:

Active Listening:
Definition and Importance: Understanding what active listening is and why it is crucial in effective communication.
Skills and Techniques: Techniques such as paraphrasing, summarizing, and asking clarifying questions to demonstrate understanding.
Non-verbal Communication: The role of body language, eye contact, and other non-verbal cues in active listening.
Barriers to Active Listening: Common obstacles that hinder effective listening and how to overcome them.
Empathy and Emotional Intelligence: How empathy and emotional intelligence contribute to active listening.
Persuasive Communication:
Definition and Purpose: What persuasive communication entails and why it is important in various contexts.
Ethos, Pathos, Logos: Understanding the persuasive appeals of credibility, emotion, and logic.

Structure and Organization: How to structure persuasive messages for maximum impact.
Audience Analysis: Tailoring persuasive communication to different audiences and their needs.
Handling Objections: Strategies for addressing and overcoming objections in persuasive communication.
Call to Action: Crafting a compelling call to action that motivates the audience to act.
Integration of Active Listening in Persuasive Communication:
Building Rapport: How active listening enhances rapport-building with the audience.
Enhanced Understanding: How understanding the audience through active listening can strengthen persuasive arguments.
Responding Effectively: Using active listening skills to respond thoughtfully to objections or concerns.
Practical Applications:
Negotiation: Applying active listening and persuasive communication techniques in negotiation scenarios.
Leadership and Management: Using these skills to lead teams effectively and influence stakeholders.
Sales and Marketing: Applying persuasive communication techniques in sales pitches and marketing campaigns.
Exercises and Case Studies:
Role-playing: Practicing active listening and persuasive communication through role-playing exercises.
Real-life Examples: Analyzing case studies of successful (or unsuccessful) persuasive communication strategies.
Overall, Chapter 22 would likely aim to equip readers with practical skills and theoretical understanding to become more effective communicators in both personal and professional contexts, emphasizing the symbiotic relationship between active listening and persuasive communication.

Chapter 23: "Leading the Way - Developing Leadership Skills," would typically cover the key qualities and attributes that contribute to effective leadership.

Here are some of the key qualities that might be discussed in such a chapter:

Visionary Thinking: Effective leaders are able to articulate a clear vision for the future and inspire others to work towards that vision.

Communication Skills: Leaders must be able to communicate effectively with their team, stakeholders, and others. This includes both speaking and listening skills.

Integrity and Ethics: Leaders should demonstrate honesty, trustworthiness, and ethical behavior in all their actions.

Empathy and Emotional Intelligence: Understanding and relating to the emotions and experiences of others, and using emotional intelligence to guide interactions and decisions.

Decision-Making Skills: Leaders need to make informed decisions in a timely manner, considering available information and potential consequences.

Strategic Thinking: Being able to think strategically and make plans that align with organizational goals and objectives.

Inspiring and Motivating: Effective leaders motivate and inspire their team members, fostering a positive and productive work environment.

Adaptability: Leaders should be adaptable and able to navigate change and uncertainty effectively.

Conflict Resolution: Being able to manage conflicts and disputes within the team or organization constructively.

Delegation and Empowerment: Knowing when and how to delegate tasks and responsibilities, and empowering team members to take ownership.

Courage and Resilience: Leaders often face challenges and setbacks; having the courage to persevere and bounce back from adversity is crucial.

Continuous Learning: Good leaders are committed to their own ongoing development and learning, staying current with industry trends and best practices.

Practical Applications:

Leadership Styles: Different leadership styles (e.g., democratic, autocratic, transformational) and when each may be appropriate.

Case Studies: Analyzing real-life examples of effective leadership and the impact of leadership decisions on organizations.

Self-Assessment: Tools and techniques for individuals to assess their own leadership strengths and areas for improvement.

Development Plans: Creating personalized development plans to enhance leadership skills over time.

Conclusion:
Chapter 23 aims to provide readers with a comprehensive understanding of the qualities that make leaders effective and equip them with practical strategies for developing and enhancing their own leadership skills. It would likely emphasize the importance of ongoing self-reflection, learning, and application of leadership principles in various professional and organizational contexts.

Chapter 24: "Transitioning from Individual Contributor to Leader: Leadership Styles and When to Use Them,"

would focus on the challenges and strategies involved in moving from a role focused on individual contributions to one that involves leading and managing others.

Here are the key points that might be covered in such a chapter:

Transitioning to Leadership:

Mindset Shift: Understanding the shift in responsibilities and mindset required when transitioning from an individual contributor to a leader.

Skills Gap Analysis: Identifying the skills and competencies needed to excel as a leader, beyond technical expertise.

Building Relationships: Establishing credibility and building effective relationships with team members, peers, and stakeholders.

Leadership Styles:
Democratic Leadership: Involving team members in decision-making processes, fostering collaboration and empowerment.

Autocratic Leadership: Making decisions independently and exerting control over team activities, suitable in crisis situations or when quick decisions are needed.

Transformational Leadership: Inspiring and motivating others through a compelling vision, encouraging innovation and growth.

Transactional Leadership: Focusing on task completion and rewarding or correcting team members based on performance.

Servant Leadership: Prioritizing the needs of others, fostering a supportive environment, and empowering team members to achieve their best.

Laissez-Faire Leadership: Allowing team members considerable freedom in decision-making and task completion, suitable for highly skilled and self-motivated teams.

When to Use Each Leadership Style:

Situational Leadership: Understanding that the effectiveness of a leadership style depends on the specific situation, including the task at hand, the team's maturity and skills, and the organizational context.

Adaptability: Knowing when to adjust leadership styles based on evolving circumstances and team dynamics.

Challenges and Strategies:
Overcoming Resistance: Addressing challenges such as resistance from former peers or adjusting to new responsibilities and expectations.

Developing Leadership Presence: Cultivating a leadership presence that commands respect and inspires confidence.

Continuous Learning: Committing to ongoing learning and development to enhance leadership skills and adapt to changing environments.

Practical Applications:
Role-Playing Exercises: Practicing different leadership styles through role-playing scenarios.

Case Studies: Analyzing real-world examples of leaders effectively applying different styles in various situations.

Feedback and Reflection: Seeking feedback from mentors, peers, and team members to assess leadership effectiveness and identify areas for improvement.

Conclusion:

Chapter 24 aims to provide practical guidance and insights for individuals making the transition from individual contributor to leader, emphasizing the importance of understanding different leadership styles and knowing when and how to apply them effectively. It would encourage readers to develop a flexible and adaptive approach to leadership, tailored to the needs of their teams and organizational goals.

Chapter 25: Building Connections

Networking for Success would delve into the significance of professional networking and its role in personal and career development.

Importance of Professional Networking:
Opportunity Creation: Networking expands your professional circle, increasing opportunities for career advancement, job prospects, and business growth.

Knowledge and Insights: Engaging with diverse professionals exposes you to new perspectives, industry trends, and valuable information.

Support and Collaboration: Networking facilitates collaboration, partnerships, and access to resources that can enhance productivity and innovation.

Career Development: Building relationships with mentors, peers, and industry leaders can provide guidance, mentorship, and career advice.

Personal Branding: Networking allows you to showcase your skills, expertise, and unique value proposition to potential employers, clients, or collaborators.

Building Confidence: Regular networking helps develop interpersonal skills, confidence in social settings, and the ability to articulate your goals and achievements effectively.

Strategies for Effective Networking:
Setting Goals: Define clear objectives for networking, such as expanding industry knowledge, seeking mentorship, or exploring career opportunities.

Attend Events and Conferences: Participate in industry-related events, conferences, seminars, and workshops to connect with professionals in your field.

Utilize Online Platforms: Leverage professional networking platforms like LinkedIn to connect with industry peers, join groups, and share insights.

Follow Up: Maintain relationships by following up with contacts after networking events, demonstrating genuine interest and willingness to collaborate.

Offer Value: Approach networking as a two-way street by offering assistance, sharing knowledge, and connecting others within your network.

Networking Etiquette: Respect networking etiquette by being genuine, respectful of others' time, and mindful of building meaningful, authentic relationships.

Overcoming Challenges:
Introversion or Shyness: Strategies for introverts to network comfortably, such as preparing talking points, setting small goals, and focusing on quality interactions.

Time Constraints: Tips for integrating networking into a busy schedule, such as prioritizing key events or using online networking opportunities.

Building Confidence: Techniques to build confidence in networking situations, such as practicing elevator pitches and seeking opportunities for gradual exposure.

Long-term Networking Strategies:
Maintain Relationships: Nurture connections over time by staying in touch, offering support, and celebrating achievements within your network.

Continual Learning: Stay updated on industry trends and developments to contribute meaningfully to professional discussions and maintain relevance.

Giving Back: Paying it forward by mentoring others, sharing opportunities, and contributing to the growth of your professional community.

Conclusion:

Chapter 25 emphasizes that professional networking is not just about collecting business cards or making superficial connections but about cultivating meaningful relationships that can support career growth and personal development. It would encourage readers to adopt a proactive approach to networking, leveraging both in-person and online platforms to build a strong and supportive professional network throughout their careers.

Chapter 26: Building and Maintaining a Strong Network.

Leveraging Networking Opportunities for Career Growth," would focus on practical strategies and tactics for effectively managing professional relationships and leveraging networking opportunities to advance one's career.

Importance of Building a Strong Network:

Access to Opportunities: How a strong network provides access to job openings, career advancement opportunities, and professional development resources.

Industry Insights and Trends: Leveraging connections to stay informed about industry trends, market changes, and emerging opportunities.

Support and Mentorship: The role of mentors, sponsors, and peers in providing guidance, advice, and support throughout different stages of your career.

Personal Branding and Reputation: How networking helps in building and enhancing your personal brand, establishing credibility, and gaining recognition in your field.

Strategies for Building a Strong Network:
Identifying Key Contacts: Identifying and connecting with individuals who can influence your career trajectory, including mentors, industry leaders, and peers.

Networking Events and Platforms: Attending industry conferences, seminars, workshops, and utilizing online platforms like LinkedIn to expand your network.

Building Genuine Relationships: Cultivating authentic relationships based on mutual trust, respect, and shared interests rather than transactional interactions.

Giving Value: Offering assistance, sharing knowledge, and providing support to others within your network to build reciprocity and goodwill.

Networking Across Hierarchies: Networking with individuals at different levels within organizations and across industries to broaden perspectives and opportunities.

Leveraging Networking Opportunities for Career Growth:
Setting Career Goals: Aligning networking efforts with specific career goals, such as securing a promotion, transitioning to a new role, or entering a different industry.

Seeking Mentorship and Guidance: Utilizing networking to identify and connect with mentors who can provide insights, advice, and career guidance.

Exploring New Roles and Opportunities: Using networking connections to explore new job opportunities, projects, collaborations, and entrepreneurial ventures.

Professional Development: Accessing learning and development opportunities, certifications, and skill-building workshops through networking contacts.

Maintaining a Strong Network:
Regular Communication: Staying in touch with contacts through emails, phone calls, meetings, and social media to nurture relationships over time.

Networking Follow-Up: Following up after networking events to express gratitude, share updates, and continue the conversation.

Engaging with Network Connections: Engaging actively in discussions, sharing insights, and participating in industry-related conversations to demonstrate expertise and maintain relevance.

Networking During Transitions: Leveraging networking during career transitions, such as job changes, relocations, or shifts in industry focus.

Overcoming Networking Challenges:
Time Management: Strategies for integrating networking into a busy schedule and prioritizing meaningful interactions.

Introversion or Shyness: Techniques for introverts to network effectively, such as preparing talking points, setting achievable goals, and focusing on quality interactions.

Conclusion:
Chapter 26 emphasizes the proactive approach to networking as an ongoing process essential for career growth and professional success. It would encourage readers to view networking not only as a means to advance their careers but also as an opportunity to contribute to their professional communities, learn from others, and build lasting relationships based on mutual respect and support.

Chapter 27: Managing Your Time

Time Management Techniques," would focus on strategies and techniques to effectively manage one's time for improved productivity and efficiency.

Understanding Time Management:
Definition and Importance: What time management entails and why it is crucial for personal and professional success.

Benefits: How effective time management leads to increased productivity, reduced stress, better work-life balance, and achievement of goals.

Time Management Techniques:
Prioritization Techniques:

Eisenhower Matrix: Prioritizing tasks based on urgency and importance.
ABC Method: Categorizing tasks into A (urgent and important), B (important but not urgent), and C (less important) categories.
Time Blocking: Allocating specific time blocks for different tasks or activities to focus on one thing at a time.
Goal Setting and Planning:

SMART Goals: Setting Specific, Measurable, Achievable, Relevant, and Time-bound goals.
Planning Techniques: Using tools like to-do lists, planners, or digital apps to plan daily, weekly, and long-term tasks.
Elimination of Time Wasters:

Identifying and Minimizing Distractions: Techniques to reduce distractions such as turning off notifications, setting boundaries, and creating a conducive work environment.
Procrastination Management: Strategies to overcome procrastination, such as breaking tasks into smaller steps and using the Pomodoro Technique (work for a set time, then take a short break).
Effective Workflow Management:

Batching Tasks: Grouping similar tasks together to minimize context-switching.
Delegation: Identifying tasks that can be delegated to others to free up time for higher-priority activities.
Time Tracking and Analysis:

Tracking Tools: Using time tracking apps or spreadsheets to monitor how time is spent.
Reflection and Adjustment: Analyzing time usage patterns to identify inefficiencies and make adjustments to improve productivity.
Integrating Time Management into Daily Routine:
Morning Routines: Establishing effective morning routines to set the tone for the day and maximize productivity.

End-of-Day Review: Reviewing accomplishments, reassessing priorities, and preparing for the next day.

Overcoming Time Management Challenges:
Overcommitment: Strategies for saying no, setting boundaries, and managing workload effectively.

Multitasking: Understanding the drawbacks of multitasking and focusing on single-tasking for better concentration and quality of work.

Personalized Time Management Strategies:
Individual Preferences: Recognizing personal peak productivity times and aligning tasks accordingly.

Continuous Improvement: Adopting a growth mindset towards improving time management skills over time.

Conclusion:
Chapter 27 emphasizes that effective time management is a skill that can be learned and improved through conscious effort and practice. It would encourage readers to identify techniques that work best for their individual preferences and circumstances, integrating them into their daily routines to achieve greater efficiency, reduce stress, and ultimately achieve their personal and professional goals.

Chapter 28: Strategies for Effective Time Management"

1. Setting Clear Goals and Priorities:
SMART Goals: Setting Specific, Measurable, Achievable, Relevant, and Time-bound goals to provide clear direction.
Prioritization Techniques: Using methods like the Eisenhower Matrix or ABC method to prioritize tasks based on urgency and importance.
2. Planning and Organization:

Daily Planning: Creating daily to-do lists or using time-blocking techniques to allocate specific time slots for tasks.
Weekly and Monthly Planning: Setting aside time to plan for longer-term objectives and projects.

3. Managing Distractions and Time Wasters:

Identifying Distractions: Recognizing common distractions and implementing strategies to minimize their impact (e.g., turning off notifications, setting boundaries).
Focus Techniques: Using techniques like the Pomodoro Technique (work for a set period, then take a short break) to maintain focus and productivity.

4. Effective Task Management:

Breaking Down Tasks: Breaking larger tasks into smaller, manageable steps to make them less overwhelming and easier to accomplish.
Using Task Management Tools: Utilizing digital tools or apps (e.g., Todoist, Trello, Asana) to track tasks, deadlines, and progress.

5. Optimizing Workflow:

Batching Similar Tasks: Grouping similar tasks together to minimize context-switching and improve efficiency.
Automation and Delegation: Automating repetitive tasks where possible and delegating tasks to others to free up time for higher-priority activities.

6. Time Tracking and Reflection:

Tracking Time: Using time tracking tools or techniques to monitor how time is spent on various activities.
Review and Adjustment: Reflecting on daily or weekly performance to identify areas for improvement and adjust strategies accordingly.

7. Improving Personal Effectiveness:

Self-Care and Energy Management: Prioritizing self-care, maintaining physical and mental well-being to sustain productivity levels.
Continuous Learning: Investing in ongoing learning and skill development to enhance efficiency and effectiveness.

8. Adapting to Challenges and Changes:
Flexibility: Being adaptable and adjusting plans in response to unexpected events or changes in priorities.
Resilience: Developing resilience to setbacks and challenges, maintaining focus on long-term goals.

9. Communication and Collaboration:
Effective Communication: Ensuring clarity in communication to avoid misunderstandings and minimize unnecessary follow-ups.
Collaboration Tools: Using collaborative tools and techniques to streamline communication and project management within teams.

10. Personalizing Strategies:
Individual Preferences: Recognizing personal strengths, peak productivity times, and preferences to tailor time management strategies accordingly.
Experimentation and Adjustment: Trying out different techniques and approaches to discover what works best and making adjustments as needed.

Conclusion:
Chapter 28 emphasizes that effective time management is a continuous process that requires deliberate planning, organization, and self-discipline. It would encourage readers to adopt a proactive approach towards managing their time, integrating various strategies and techniques into their daily routines to optimize productivity, achieve goals, and maintain a healthy work-life balance.

Chapter 29: Prioritizing Tasks and Avoiding Procrastination.

Understanding Prioritization:
Importance of Prioritization:

Discussing why prioritization is crucial for productivity, goal achievement, and stress management.
Methods of Prioritization:

Eisenhower Matrix: Sorting tasks based on urgency and importance.

ABC Method: Categorizing tasks into A (high priority), B (medium priority), and C (low priority).

Time Management Grids: Tools to visualize and prioritize tasks based on their impact and effort required.

Techniques for Prioritizing Tasks:

Setting Clear Goals:

Using SMART goals (Specific, Measurable, Achievable, Relevant, Time-bound) to clarify objectives and prioritize tasks accordingly.

Daily Planning:

Creating to-do lists or using time-blocking techniques to allocate time for high-priority tasks.

Chunking and Breaking Down Tasks:

Breaking larger tasks into smaller, manageable steps to facilitate progress and reduce overwhelm.

Strategies to Avoid Procrastination:

Understanding Procrastination:

Exploring common causes of procrastination, such as fear of failure, perfectionism, or lack of motivation.

Overcoming Procrastination:

Eat That Frog: Tackling the most challenging task first thing in the morning.

Pomodoro Technique: Working in focused intervals (e.g., 25 minutes of work followed by a short break) to maintain momentum.

Task Visualization: Visualizing the desired outcome of completing a task to increase motivation and reduce procrastination.

Creating Accountability:

Sharing goals and deadlines with colleagues, mentors, or friends to create external accountability.

Minimizing Distractions:

Identifying and eliminating or reducing distractions (e.g., turning off notifications, setting dedicated work periods).

Developing a Productive Mindset:

Mindfulness and Self-Reflection:

Practicing mindfulness to stay present and focused on tasks. Reflecting on progress and adjusting strategies to improve productivity and time management.

Building Habits:

Establishing routines and habits that support effective task prioritization and time management.

Overcoming Challenges:

Perseverance and Resilience:

Developing resilience to setbacks and maintaining motivation during challenging tasks.

Continuous Improvement:

Embracing a growth mindset to continually refine prioritization and time management skills.

Personalizing Strategies:

Understanding Personal Productivity Peaks:

Identifying peak times of productivity and scheduling high-priority tasks during these periods.

Experimentation and Adaptation:

Trying out different techniques and adjusting strategies based on individual preferences and feedback.

Conclusion:

Chapter 29 emphasizes that effective task prioritization and overcoming procrastination are skills that can be developed with practice and persistence. It would provide readers with practical tools and insights to enhance their ability to manage tasks efficiently, maintain focus, and achieve greater productivity in both professional and personal endeavors.

Chapter 30: Balancing Workload to Prevent Burnout.

Understanding Burnout:
Definition and Symptoms:

Defining burnout and discussing its symptoms, such as chronic fatigue, cynicism, and reduced professional efficacy.
Causes of Burnout:

Exploring common causes of burnout, including high workload, lack of control, insufficient support, and unclear job expectations.

Importance of Work-Life Balance:

Benefits of Balance:

Discussing the benefits of a balanced life, such as improved mental and physical health, increased job satisfaction, and higher productivity.

Impact of Imbalance:

Exploring the negative effects of an unbalanced life, including stress, decreased motivation, and strained relationships.

Strategies for Balancing Workload:

Setting Boundaries:

Establishing clear boundaries between work and personal life, such as defining work hours and limiting after-hours communication.

Prioritization and Time Management:

Using effective prioritization techniques (e.g., Eisenhower Matrix, ABC method) and time management strategies to manage workload efficiently.

Delegation and Collaboration:

Delegating tasks to team members or seeking assistance when workload is overwhelming.

Fostering collaboration to share responsibilities and leverage team strengths.

Stress Management Techniques:

Mindfulness and Relaxation:

Practicing mindfulness techniques, meditation, or deep breathing exercises to reduce stress and promote relaxation.

Physical Well-being:

Prioritizing physical health through regular exercise, nutritious diet, and adequate sleep to enhance resilience against stress.

Creating a Supportive Work Environment:

Communication and Feedback:

Encouraging open communication and feedback channels to address workload concerns and promote a supportive culture.

Professional Development:

Providing opportunities for skill development, training, and growth to empower employees and reduce feelings of overwhelm.

Recognizing and Addressing Signs of Burnout:

Self-Assessment:

Encouraging individuals to regularly assess their own well-being and recognize early signs of burnout.

Seeking Support:

Encouraging individuals to seek support from colleagues, mentors, or professional resources if experiencing symptoms of burnout.

Cultivating Work-Life Integration:

Flexibility and Adaptability:

Promoting flexible work arrangements and adaptive policies that support work-life integration and individual needs.

Personal Reflection and Adjustment:

Encouraging individuals to reflect on their priorities and make adjustments to achieve a sustainable balance over time.

Conclusion:

Chapter 30 emphasizes the proactive approach to managing workload and maintaining a healthy work-life balance as essential for preventing burnout. It would provide practical strategies and resources to help individuals and organizations create supportive environments that prioritize well-being, resilience, and sustained performance. By fostering a culture that values balance and supports personal well-being, readers can mitigate the risks of burnout and cultivate long-term professional satisfaction and success.

Chapter 31: Acing the Interview

Mastering Interviewing Skills," would focus on preparing individuals to excel in job interviews by mastering essential skills and strategies.

Preparing for the Interview:
Researching the Company:

Gathering information about the company's mission, values, products/services, culture, and recent news.
Understanding the Job Description:

Analyzing the job requirements, responsibilities, and qualifications to align responses with the employer's needs.
Preparing Responses to Common Questions:

Anticipating and rehearsing answers to typical interview questions, including behavioral questions (e.g., "Tell me about a time when...") and technical questions related to the role.
Developing Questions to Ask the Interviewer:

Formulating thoughtful questions about the position, team dynamics, company culture, and opportunities for growth to demonstrate interest and engagement.
Mastering Interview Techniques:
Body Language and Non-verbal Communication:

Practicing positive body language (e.g., eye contact, posture, gestures) to convey confidence and professionalism.
Active Listening:

Demonstrating attentive listening skills by paraphrasing questions, maintaining focus, and asking relevant follow-up questions.
Effective Communication:

Articulating responses clearly and concisely, emphasizing relevant skills, experiences, and achievements.
Building Rapport:

Establishing rapport with interviewers through genuine interest, enthusiasm, and a professional demeanor.
Handling Different Types of Interviews:

Behavioral Interviews:

Structuring responses using the STAR method (Situation, Task, Action, Result) to provide concrete examples of past accomplishments and skills.

Technical Interviews:

Preparing for technical assessments or questions specific to the role, showcasing expertise and problem-solving abilities.

Panel Interviews:

Engaging with multiple interviewers by addressing each person while maintaining a cohesive narrative.

Managing Stress and Nerves:

Pre-interview Preparation:

Techniques for managing pre-interview anxiety, such as practicing deep breathing, visualization, or positive affirmations.

Confidence-Building Strategies:

Recalling past successes, focusing on strengths, and maintaining a positive mindset throughout the interview process.

Post-Interview Follow-up:

Sending Thank-You Notes:

Crafting personalized thank-you emails to express appreciation for the opportunity and reiterate interest in the position.

Reflecting on the Interview:

Reflecting on the interview experience to identify areas of strength and opportunities for improvement in future interviews.

Special Considerations:

Virtual Interviews:

Tips for navigating virtual interviews, including ensuring technical setup, maintaining eye contact, and minimizing distractions.

Second-round Interviews:

Strategies for preparing for follow-up interviews, including building on previous discussions and demonstrating continued interest and qualifications.

Conclusion:

Chapter 31 equips readers with the knowledge, skills, and confidence needed to excel in job interviews. By mastering interview techniques, understanding the employer's perspective, and effectively communicating their qualifications, readers can increase their chances of securing their desired roles and advancing their careers. The chapter would emphasize the importance of thorough preparation, professionalism, and continuous learning to consistently perform well in interview settings.

Chapter 32: Preparing for Different Types of Interviews, Common Interview Questions, and Following Up After the Interview.

1. Types of Interviews:
a. Behavioral Interviews:
Definition: Explaining the structure where candidates discuss past experiences using the STAR method (Situation, Task, Action, Result).
Preparation: Providing examples aligned with job requirements.
Example Questions: Detailing questions like "Tell me about a time when you faced a challenge and how you overcame it."
b. Technical Interviews:
Purpose: Discussing assessments related to technical skills or knowledge.
Preparation: Preparing for coding challenges, case studies, or technical questions.
Example Questions: Examples such as "Walk me through your approach to solving [specific technical problem]."
c. Panel Interviews:
Description: Describing interviews involving multiple interviewers.
Approach: Strategies for engaging with each panel member and addressing diverse perspectives.

Example Questions: Addressing questions from different panel members and maintaining consistency in responses.

2. Common Interview Questions:

a. Traditional Questions:

Examples: Providing examples such as "Tell me about yourself" and "What are your strengths and weaknesses?"

Responses: Structuring concise, relevant answers that highlight skills and experiences.

b. Competency-Based Questions:

Examples: Detailing questions such as "Give me an example of a time when you showed leadership."

STAR Method: Explaining how to structure responses using Situation, Task, Action, and Result.

c. Situational Questions:

Examples: Including questions like "How would you handle a conflict with a team member?"

Approach: Outlining strategies for presenting hypothetical scenarios and demonstrating problem-solving skills.

3. Following Up After the Interview:

a. Thank-You Notes:

Purpose: Explaining the importance of expressing appreciation and reiterating interest.

Timing: Providing guidance on sending personalized emails within 24-48 hours.

b. Additional Follow-Up:

Post-Interview Communication: Addressing potential follow-up questions or providing additional information.

Professionalism: Emphasizing professionalism and respect for the interviewer's time.

Conclusion:

Chapter 32 equips readers with practical knowledge and strategies to excel in various interview formats, navigate common interview questions effectively, and conduct professional follow-up. By preparing thoroughly, demonstrating competence and confidence during interviews, and maintaining courteous follow-up, individuals can enhance their prospects of securing job offers and advancing their careers. The chapter would underscore the importance of continuous improvement and learning from each interview experience to refine skills and strategies further.

Chapter 33: Crafting Your Narrative - Effective Resume Writing.

1. Understanding the Purpose of a Resume:
Definition: Clarifying the role of a resume as a marketing tool to showcase qualifications and suitability for a specific job.
Key Objectives: Outlining goals such as securing interviews, highlighting relevant skills, and differentiating from other candidates.
2. Components of an Effective Resume:
a. Contact Information:
Essential Details: Including name, phone number, email address, and LinkedIn profile (if applicable).
Professional Email Address: Advising on using a professional email address.
b. Resume Summary or Objective Statement:
Purpose: Summarizing professional background, skills, and career goals.

Tailoring to Job: Customizing to align with the specific job role and employer's needs.

c. Professional Experience:

Job Descriptions: Detailing past employment roles, responsibilities, and achievements using concise bullet points.

Quantifiable Achievements: Emphasizing accomplishments with metrics or results whenever possible.

Relevance: Highlighting experiences most relevant to the target position.

d. Education:

Degrees and Certifications: Listing academic qualifications, degrees, and relevant certifications.

Honors and Awards: Including any academic or professional awards.

e. Skills:

Technical and Soft Skills: Enumerating skills relevant to the job, such as technical proficiencies and soft skills like communication or leadership.

Keywords: Incorporating industry-specific keywords to pass applicant tracking systems (ATS) and attract recruiters' attention.

3. Formatting and Design:

a. Layout:

Clean and Readable Format: Choosing a professional layout with clear headings and bullet points for easy readability.

Consistency: Ensuring consistency in font size, style, and formatting throughout the resume.

b. Length:

Optimal Length: Recommending a concise resume (usually 1-2 pages) that highlights key qualifications and achievements.

Trimming Unnecessary Details: Editing out irrelevant information to maintain focus on relevant experiences.

4. Tailoring Your Resume to Specific Roles:

Customization: Adapting the resume to match the job description and emphasize relevant skills and experiences.

Research: Conducting research on the company and position to align the resume with employer expectations.

5. Proofreading and Review:

Editing: Reviewing for grammar, spelling errors, and consistency.

Feedback: Seeking feedback from peers, mentors, or career advisors to ensure clarity and effectiveness.

6. Using Action Verbs and Quantifiable Metrics:

Action-Oriented Language: Starting bullet points with strong action verbs (e.g., managed, developed, implemented).

Metrics: Including quantifiable achievements and results to demonstrate impact.

7. Digital Presence and Online Resumes:

LinkedIn Profile: Integrating LinkedIn profiles and optimizing for consistency with the resume.

Online Portfolios: Linking to portfolios or personal websites showcasing relevant work samples.

Conclusion:

Chapter 33 emphasizes that crafting an effective resume requires strategic thinking, attention to detail, and a clear understanding of one's professional narrative. By following the guidelines provided, individuals can create a compelling resume that not only highlights their qualifications and achievements but also resonates with hiring managers and recruiters. The chapter would encourage continuous refinement and customization of resumes to match specific job opportunities and maximize chances of securing interviews and advancing in their careers.

Chapter 34: Key Elements of a Standout Resume, Tailoring Your Resume for Specific Roles, and Avoiding Common Resume Mistakes

1. Key Elements of a Standout Resume:
a. Resume Summary or Objective Statement:
Purpose: Summarizing career goals, key skills, and experience in a concise manner.
Impactful Introduction: Crafting a compelling opening to grab the recruiter's attention immediately.
b. Professional Experience:
Relevant Experience: Highlighting past roles and responsibilities that align with the target job.

Achievements: Using bullet points to showcase quantifiable achievements and contributions.

c. Education and Certifications:

Degrees and Institutions: Listing educational qualifications relevant to the job.

Certifications and Training: Including certifications or professional training that add value to the resume.

d. Skills:

Technical and Soft Skills: Enumerating relevant skills that match the job description.

Keyword Optimization: Incorporating industry-specific keywords to pass through applicant tracking systems (ATS).

e. Achievements and Awards:

Honors: Mentioning any professional awards or recognition received.

Projects: Highlighting significant projects or initiatives that demonstrate skills and capabilities.

2. Tailoring Your Resume for Specific Roles:

a. Job Description Analysis:

Understanding Requirements: Analyzing the job description to identify key skills and qualifications sought by the employer.

Highlighting Relevant Experience: Tailoring the resume to emphasize experiences and achievements most relevant to the specific role.

b. Customizing Resume Sections:

Objective Statement: Modifying the resume summary or objective statement to align with the job applied for.

Professional Experience: Rearranging and prioritizing past experiences to showcase the most relevant ones first.

3. Avoiding Common Resume Mistakes:

a. Formatting and Design:

Consistency: Ensuring consistent formatting throughout the resume.

Clutter: Avoiding excessive use of design elements that may distract from content.

b. Content Errors:
Spelling and Grammar: Proofreading for spelling and grammatical errors.
Accuracy: Verifying dates, job titles, and contact information for accuracy.
c. Generic Resumes:
One-Size-Fits-All Approach: Tailoring resumes for specific roles instead of using a generic template.
Lack of Focus: Ensuring each section of the resume contributes directly to showcasing qualifications for the job.
d. Overuse of Jargon or Buzzwords:
Clarity: Using clear and straightforward language to communicate skills and achievements.
Avoiding Clichés: Steer clear of overused phrases that may sound generic or insincere.

4. Conclusion:

Chapter 34 emphasizes the importance of creating a standout resume that effectively communicates skills, experiences, and achievements tailored to specific job opportunities. By understanding the key elements of an effective resume, customizing it to match job descriptions, and avoiding common mistakes, individuals can significantly enhance their chances of securing interviews and advancing in their careers. The chapter would encourage continuous improvement and adaptation of resumes based on feedback and evolving career goals, ensuring they remain competitive in the job market.

Chapter 35: Embracing Change - Navigating Career Transitions

1. Understanding Career Transitions:
a. Definition and Types of Transitions:
Definition: Explaining career transitions as shifts in employment status, industry, or role.
Types: Discussing transitions such as job changes, promotions, career shifts, and re-entering the workforce.
b. Reasons for Career Transitions:
Professional Growth: Pursuing new challenges, skills development, or career advancement.
Personal Factors: Responding to changes in personal circumstances or interests.
2. Assessing Career Goals and Values:
a. Self-Assessment:

Skills and Strengths: Evaluating current skills and strengths.
Interests and Passions: Identifying career interests and passions.

b. Goal Setting:

Short-Term and Long-Term Goals: Setting realistic and achievable career goals.
SMART Goals: Applying the SMART criteria (Specific, Measurable, Achievable, Relevant, Time-bound) to goal setting.

3. Planning and Preparation for Transitions:

a. Researching Options:

Exploring Opportunities: Researching industries, companies, and roles aligned with career goals.
Networking: Leveraging professional networks for insights and opportunities.

b. Skill Development:

Identifying Gaps: Assessing skills needed for the desired role or industry.
Training and Education: Pursuing courses, certifications, or training programs to acquire necessary skills.

4. Managing Change and Adaptability:

a. Embracing Uncertainty:

Resilience: Building resilience to navigate uncertainties and setbacks.
Flexibility: Remaining open to new opportunities and possibilities.

b. Overcoming Challenges:

Addressing Fear and Resistance: Managing fear of change and overcoming resistance to transition.
Seeking Support: Seeking mentorship, coaching, or counseling for guidance and encouragement.

5. Practical Steps During Career Transitions:

a. Updating Resume and LinkedIn Profile:

Highlighting Relevant Experience: Tailoring resume and profile to reflect skills and experiences relevant to new career goals.

Networking: Engaging with contacts and connections to explore new opportunities.

b. Interview Preparation:

Research and Preparation: Researching prospective employers and preparing for interviews.

Demonstrating Transferable Skills: Showcasing transferable skills and experiences during interviews.

6. Financial Considerations:

a. Budgeting and Planning:

Financial Stability: Planning for potential changes in income or expenses during transitions.

Saving and Investment: Managing finances to support career changes and new opportunities.

7. Psychological and Emotional Well-being:

a. Self-Care:

Stress Management: Practicing self-care techniques to manage stress and maintain well-being.

Mindfulness: Incorporating mindfulness practices to stay grounded during transitions.

8. Evaluating and Reflecting:

a. Monitoring Progress:

Assessment: Reflecting on progress towards career goals and adjusting strategies as needed.

Learning and Growth: Embracing learning opportunities and continuous improvement.

Conclusion:

Chapter 35 encourages individuals to embrace change as an opportunity for growth and development in their careers. By assessing goals, planning effectively, building resilience, and seeking support, individuals can successfully navigate career transitions and achieve fulfillment in their professional lives. The chapter would emphasize the importance of adaptability, continuous learning, and maintaining a positive mindset throughout the transition process, ensuring readiness for future career opportunities and challenges.

Chapter 36: Identifying When It's Time for a Career Change, Planning and Executing a Successful Career Transition, and Overcoming Challenges During a Career Shift

1. Recognizing the Need for a Career Change:
a. Signs and Indicators:

Lack of Passion: Feeling unfulfilled or lacking enthusiasm for current work.
Skills Mismatch: Recognizing that current skills and strengths are not fully utilized.
Job Dissatisfaction: Experiencing persistent dissatisfaction or stress related to current job responsibilities.
Career Plateau: Feeling stagnant with limited opportunities for growth or advancement.
b. Self-Assessment:
Values and Interests: Assessing personal values, interests, and career aspirations.
Skills and Strengths: Evaluating strengths and skills that can be leveraged in a new career path.
Career Goals: Identifying long-term career goals and aspirations.
2. Planning and Executing a Successful Career Transition:
a. Research and Exploration:
Industry and Role Research: Exploring potential industries, companies, and roles aligned with career interests.
Networking: Utilizing professional networks to gather insights, advice, and job opportunities.
Skill Development: Identifying and acquiring necessary skills through training, certifications, or further education.
b. Goal Setting and Action Plan:
SMART Goals: Setting Specific, Measurable, Achievable, Relevant, and Time-bound goals for the career transition.
Timeline: Creating a timeline with actionable steps and milestones for achieving career transition goals.
3. Overcoming Challenges During a Career Shift:
a. Financial Considerations:
Budgeting: Planning for potential changes in income and expenses during the transition period.
Savings and Safety Net: Building financial reserves to support career change and mitigate risks.
b. Psychological and Emotional Well-being:

Managing Uncertainty: Developing resilience to cope with uncertainties and setbacks during the transition.

Self-Care: Prioritizing self-care practices to maintain mental and emotional health throughout the process.

c. Skill and Experience Transfer:

Identifying Transferable Skills: Recognizing and highlighting skills and experiences that are relevant and transferable to the new career path.

Addressing Skill Gaps: Pursuing training or development opportunities to bridge skill gaps necessary for the new role.

4. Networking and Support:

a. Building Relationships:

Networking Strategies: Engaging with mentors, industry professionals, and peers for guidance and support.

Professional Associations: Joining relevant associations or groups to expand networks and access career resources.

b. Seeking Mentorship and Guidance:

Career Coaches: Consulting with career coaches or counselors for personalized guidance and advice.

Peer Support: Leveraging support from friends, family, or peers who can provide encouragement and perspective.

5. Evaluating Progress and Adjusting:

a. Monitoring Success:

Assessment: Regularly evaluating progress towards career transition goals and adjusting strategies as needed.

Learning and Adaptation: Embracing learning opportunities and adapting to changing circumstances throughout the transition.

Conclusion:

Chapter 36 empowers individuals to recognize when a career change is necessary, plan effectively for the transition, and navigate challenges with resilience and determination. By focusing on self-assessment, goal setting, skill development, and leveraging support networks, individuals can successfully navigate career shifts and achieve meaningful professional growth and satisfaction. The chapter would underscore the importance of proactive planning, continuous learning, and maintaining a positive mindset to overcome obstacles and seize new career opportunities.

Chapter 37: Balancing Act - Achieving Work-Life Balance

1. Understanding Work-Life Balance:
a. Definition and Importance:
Definition: Explaining work-life balance as the harmony between professional obligations and personal life.
Significance: Discussing the benefits of work-life balance for mental health, productivity, and overall well-being.
b. Common Challenges:
Workplace Culture: Addressing pressures and expectations that may impact work-life balance.
Technology and Connectivity: Managing the blurring boundaries between work and personal life due to digital connectivity.
2. Strategies for Achieving Work-Life Balance:
a. Setting Boundaries:
Establishing Clear Boundaries: Defining specific work hours and non-negotiable personal time.
Technology Use: Implementing practices like turning off work notifications during non-work hours.
b. Time Management:
Prioritization: Using techniques such as prioritization grids or to-do lists to manage tasks effectively.
Time Blocking: Allocating dedicated time slots for work, personal activities, and relaxation.
c. Stress Management:
Mindfulness and Relaxation: Practicing mindfulness techniques, meditation, or deep breathing exercises to reduce stress.
Physical Well-being: Prioritizing regular exercise, nutritious diet, and sufficient sleep to enhance resilience against stress.
3. Nurturing Personal Relationships:
a. Family and Social Connections:
Quality Time: Allocating time for family activities, socializing with friends, and maintaining meaningful relationships.
Communication: Openly discussing work commitments and seeking support from loved ones.
4. Professional Development and Growth:

a. Career Satisfaction:
Alignment with Values: Pursuing roles and opportunities that align with personal values and interests.
Skill Enhancement: Investing in continuous learning and professional development to enhance job satisfaction and growth.

5. Flexibility and Adaptability:

a. Flexible Work Arrangements:
Telecommuting and Remote Work: Negotiating flexible work schedules or remote work options when feasible.
Workplace Policies: Understanding and leveraging organizational policies that support work-life balance.

6. Self-Care and Well-being:

a. Mental and Emotional Health:
Self-Care Practices: Incorporating activities such as hobbies, relaxation, or therapy to maintain mental and emotional well-being.
Workplace Support: Utilizing employee assistance programs or counseling services for additional support.

7. Evaluating and Adjusting:

a. Reflection:
Assessment: Reflecting on current work-life balance and identifying areas for improvement.
Feedback: Seeking feedback from colleagues, mentors, or loved ones on work-life balance effectiveness.

Conclusion:
Chapter 37 emphasizes the importance of intentional efforts to achieve and maintain work-life balance amidst professional demands. By implementing strategies for boundary-setting, time management, stress reduction, and nurturing personal relationships, individuals can cultivate a balanced lifestyle that supports both career success and personal fulfillment. The chapter would encourage ongoing self-assessment, adaptation to changing circumstances, and prioritization of well-being to sustain long-term satisfaction and productivity in both professional and personal domains.

Chapter 38: Importance of Work-Life Balance for Long-Term Success, Strategies for Managing Work and Personal Life, Setting Boundaries, and Making Time for Self-Care

1. Importance of Work-Life Balance for Long-Term Success:
a. Health and Well-being:
Physical Health: Discussing how balanced lifestyles contribute to reduced stress levels, better sleep patterns, and overall physical health.
Mental Health: Exploring the impact of work-life balance on mental well-being, including reduced burnout and improved emotional resilience.
b. Productivity and Performance:
Enhanced Focus: How adequate rest and personal time foster increased concentration and productivity during work hours.
Creativity and Innovation: Discussing how balanced lifestyles stimulate creativity and innovation, leading to improved problem-solving abilities.
c. Career Satisfaction:
Job Satisfaction: Exploring how balanced lifestyles contribute to higher job satisfaction and lower turnover rates.

Professional Growth: Discussing how personal fulfillment outside of work positively impacts career development and long-term career success.

2. Strategies for Managing Work and Personal Life:

a. Time Management:

Prioritization: Strategies for prioritizing tasks and responsibilities to ensure both work and personal commitments are met.

Time Blocking: Implementing time-blocking techniques to allocate dedicated time for work, family, hobbies, and self-care.

b. Setting Boundaries:

Work Boundaries: Establishing clear boundaries between work and personal life, including setting specific work hours and avoiding after-hours work emails or calls.

Personal Boundaries: Discussing the importance of protecting personal time for relaxation, hobbies, and family activities.

3. Making Time for Self-Care:

a. Physical Self-Care:

Exercise and Nutrition: Strategies for incorporating regular exercise and maintaining a balanced diet despite busy schedules.

Rest and Recovery: Importance of adequate sleep and relaxation techniques to recharge and prevent burnout.

b. Mental and Emotional Self-Care:

Stress Management: Techniques for managing stress levels, including mindfulness, meditation, or journaling.

Personal Growth: Importance of pursuing personal interests, hobbies, and learning opportunities outside of work.

4. Communication and Support Systems:

a. Family and Social Support:

Open Communication: Strategies for discussing work-life balance needs with family members and loved ones.

Shared Responsibilities: Importance of sharing household and family responsibilities to alleviate pressure on individuals.

b. Workplace Support:

Company Policies: Leveraging workplace policies that support work-life balance, such as flexible work arrangements or wellness programs.

Peer Support: Building supportive relationships with colleagues to foster a positive work environment and mutual understanding of work-life balance needs.

5. Evaluating and Adjusting:

a. Regular Assessment:

Reflection: Encouraging individuals to periodically reflect on their work-life balance and make adjustments as needed.

Feedback: Seeking feedback from trusted sources, such as mentors or supervisors, on work-life balance effectiveness and areas for improvement.

Conclusion:

Chapter 38 emphasizes that achieving and maintaining work-life balance is crucial for long-term success, well-being, and overall satisfaction in both professional and personal domains. By implementing effective strategies for managing time, setting boundaries, prioritizing self-care, and fostering supportive relationships, individuals can cultivate a balanced lifestyle that promotes health, happiness, and sustained productivity throughout their careers. The chapter would underscore the importance of proactive self-management, continuous improvement, and advocating for work-life balance in organizational cultures to ensure sustainable success and fulfillment.

Chapter 39: Setting the Stage - Goal Setting for Professional Growth

1. Importance of Goal Setting in Professional Growth:
a. Clarity and Direction:
Defining Objectives: Clarifying career aspirations and long-term objectives.
Motivation: Discussing how goals provide motivation and focus for career development efforts.
b. Progress Tracking:
Measurable Outcomes: Setting goals with measurable criteria to track progress and achievements.
Accountability: Holding oneself accountable for achieving set goals within specified timelines.
2. Types of Professional Goals:
a. Short-Term Goals:
Immediate Objectives: Setting goals that can be achieved within weeks or months.
Skill Development: Goals focused on acquiring new skills or improving existing ones.
b. Long-Term Goals:
Career Milestones: Setting ambitious goals for career advancement or achieving specific positions.
Personal Growth: Goals aimed at personal growth and development over an extended period.
3. SMART Goal Framework:
a. Specific:

Clear Objectives: Setting specific and well-defined goals that focus on particular outcomes or achievements.

b. Measurable:
Quantifiable Criteria: Establishing criteria to measure progress and success.

c. Achievable:
Realistic Goals: Setting goals that are challenging yet attainable based on skills, resources, and timeframe.

d. Relevant:
Alignment with Objectives: Ensuring goals align with career aspirations and organizational objectives.

e. Time-Bound:
Defined Timeline: Setting deadlines or milestones to create a sense of urgency and accountability.

4. Steps to Effective Goal Setting:

a. Self-Assessment:
Strengths and Weaknesses: Evaluating current skills, strengths, and areas for improvement.
Career Aspirations: Identifying long-term career aspirations and goals.

b. Prioritization:
Ranking Goals: Prioritizing goals based on importance and potential impact on career growth.
Short-term vs. Long-term: Balancing immediate needs with long-term career objectives.

5. Strategies for Achieving Professional Goals:

a. Action Planning:
Breaking Down Goals: Breaking down goals into actionable steps and tasks.
Setting Milestones: Establishing milestones to track progress towards larger objectives.

b. Continuous Learning:
Skill Development: Pursuing opportunities for training, certifications, or workshops to enhance skills.
Feedback and Reflection: Seeking feedback and reflecting on experiences to refine goals and strategies.

6. Overcoming Challenges in Goal Achievement:
a. Time Management:
Prioritizing Tasks: Balancing daily responsibilities with goal-focused activities.
Adaptability: Adjusting goals and strategies in response to changing circumstances or setbacks.
b. Motivation and Persistence:
Staying Focused: Maintaining motivation and enthusiasm throughout the goal pursuit process.
Resilience: Building resilience to overcome obstacles and setbacks encountered along the way.
7. Reviewing and Adjusting Goals:
a. Regular Evaluation:
Assessment: Periodically reviewing progress towards goals and adjusting strategies as needed.
Celebrating Success: Recognizing achievements and milestones to maintain momentum and motivation.
Conclusion:
Chapter 39 underscores the importance of setting clear, SMART goals for professional growth and career advancement. By following structured approaches to goal setting, individuals can enhance their focus, motivation, and accountability in achieving career objectives. The chapter would encourage continuous learning, adaptation to change, and proactive self-management to foster long-term success and fulfillment in professional endeavors.

Chapter 40: Techniques for Setting and Achieving Professional Goals, Creating Short-Term and Long-Term Career Plans, Evaluating and Adjusting Goals as Needed

1. Techniques for Setting and Achieving Professional Goals:
a. Goal Setting Techniques:
SMART Goals: Detailed explanation of setting goals that are Specific, Measurable, Achievable, Relevant, and Time-bound.
Stretch Goals: Setting ambitious goals to push beyond current capabilities.
Outcome-based Goals: Focusing on desired outcomes and results.
b. Visioning and Visualization:
Creating a Vision: Imagining the desired future state of one's career.
Visualization Techniques: Using visualization exercises to reinforce motivation and focus.
2. Creating Short-Term and Long-Term Career Plans:
a. Short-Term Career Plans:

Immediate Objectives: Setting short-term goals to achieve within the next few months or year.
Skill Development: Planning for acquiring new skills or enhancing existing ones.
b. Long-Term Career Plans:
Career Aspirations: Setting long-term goals for career advancement or achieving specific milestones.
Personal Growth: Planning for continuous professional development and career progression over several years.
3. Evaluating and Adjusting Goals as Needed:
a. Regular Assessment:
Progress Tracking: Monitoring progress towards goals and assessing achievements.
Feedback and Reflection: Seeking feedback from mentors, supervisors, or peers to evaluate performance and adjust goals accordingly.
b. Adapting to Changes:
Environmental Changes: Adjusting goals in response to changes in the industry, organization, or personal circumstances.
Revising Strategies: Modifying action plans and strategies to align with evolving career goals and priorities.
4. Strategies for Achieving Professional Goals:
a. Action Planning:
Breaking Down Goals: Breaking down larger goals into smaller, manageable tasks and action steps.
Setting Deadlines: Establishing deadlines and milestones to maintain accountability and track progress.
b. Continuous Learning:
Skill Enhancement: Pursuing professional development opportunities, such as courses, workshops, or certifications.
Networking: Building relationships and connections to leverage career opportunities and support goal achievement.
5. Overcoming Challenges in Goal Achievement:
a. Time Management:

Prioritization: Balancing work responsibilities, personal commitments, and goal-focused activities.

Efficiency Strategies: Implementing time management techniques to maximize productivity and focus.

b. Motivation and Persistence:

Maintaining Motivation: Strategies for staying motivated and enthusiastic throughout the goal pursuit process.

Resilience: Building resilience to overcome setbacks and obstacles encountered along the way.

6. Reviewing and Adjusting Goals:

a. Regular Evaluation:

Assessment: Periodically reviewing progress towards goals and assessing effectiveness of strategies.

Celebrate Milestones: Recognizing achievements and milestones to maintain motivation and momentum.

Conclusion:

Chapter 40 emphasizes the importance of strategic goal setting, planning, and continuous evaluation in achieving professional success and career satisfaction. By implementing effective techniques for goal setting, creating comprehensive career plans, and regularly reviewing and adapting goals, individuals can enhance their focus, productivity, and overall career trajectory. The chapter would encourage proactive self-management, learning from experiences, and leveraging support networks to navigate challenges and seize opportunities for professional growth and advancement.

Chapter 41: Thriving in the Workplace - Understanding Workplace Culture

1. Importance of Workplace Culture in Career Satisfaction:
a. Definition of Workplace Culture:
Core Values and Beliefs: Defining the shared values, norms, and behaviors that characterize the organization.
Impact on Employees: Discussing how workplace culture influences employee engagement, motivation, and job satisfaction.
b. Alignment with Personal Values:
Cultural Fit: Importance of aligning personal values and work ethics with organizational culture for long-term career satisfaction.
Organizational Values: Recognizing and assessing organizational values during the job search and career progression.
2. Navigating and Adapting to Different Workplace Cultures:
a. Cultural Awareness:

Understanding Diversity: Emphasizing the diversity of workplace cultures and the importance of cultural sensitivity.
Observation and Adaptation: Techniques for observing and adapting to different workplace norms and practices.
b. Flexibility and Openness:
Adapting Communication Styles: Adjusting communication approaches to fit the cultural context of the organization.
Embracing Change: Being open to change and embracing opportunities to learn from diverse workplace cultures.
3. Contributing Positively to Workplace Culture:
a. Collaboration and Teamwork:
Building Relationships: Developing positive relationships with colleagues and fostering a collaborative work environment.
Respect and Inclusivity: Promoting respect, inclusivity, and diversity within the workplace culture.
b. Leadership and Initiative:
Taking Initiative: Demonstrating leadership by taking initiative in projects and contributing innovative ideas.
Supporting Cultural Values: Aligning personal actions with organizational values and promoting them through leadership.
4. Addressing Challenges in Workplace Culture:
a. Conflict Resolution:
Managing Conflict: Strategies for resolving conflicts respectfully and constructively within different cultural contexts.
Seeking Guidance: Knowing when and how to seek guidance from supervisors or HR professionals for cultural challenges.
b. Continuous Improvement:
Feedback and Adaptation: Using feedback to continuously improve interactions and contributions to workplace culture.
Learning and Development: Pursuing professional development opportunities to enhance cultural competence and leadership skills.
5. Creating a Positive Work Environment:

a. Well-being and Support:

Promoting Well-being: Supporting initiatives that enhance employee well-being, such as work-life balance programs and wellness activities.

Recognition and Appreciation: Celebrating achievements and acknowledging contributions to reinforce positive workplace culture.

6. Conclusion:

Chapter 41 highlights the pivotal role of workplace culture in shaping career satisfaction and professional growth. By understanding, adapting to, and positively contributing to diverse workplace cultures, individuals can foster meaningful connections, enhance productivity, and create a supportive environment conducive to personal and organizational success. The chapter would encourage proactive engagement, cultural awareness, and continuous efforts to align personal values with organizational culture for sustained career fulfillment and advancement.

Chapter 42: The Art of Negotiation - Developing Negotiation Skills

1. Key Principles of Effective Negotiation:
a. Preparation:
Understanding Goals: Clarifying objectives and desired outcomes before entering negotiations.
Research: Gathering information about the negotiation topic, counterparts, and potential alternatives.
b. Communication:
Active Listening: Listening actively to understand the other party's perspective and concerns.
Clear Communication: Articulating one's position clearly and persuasively during negotiations.
c. Collaboration:
Win-Win Solutions: Seeking mutually beneficial agreements that satisfy both parties' interests.
Building Relationships: Fostering positive relationships and trust during negotiations.
d. Problem-Solving:
Creative Solutions: Generating innovative solutions to overcome obstacles and reach agreements.

Managing Conflicts: Addressing conflicts constructively to maintain progress in negotiations.

2. Preparing for Salary Negotiations and Other Workplace Negotiations:

a. Salary Negotiations:

Know Your Worth: Researching market rates and industry standards for the position.

Quantify Achievements: Highlighting past accomplishments and contributions to justify salary expectations.

Benefits and Perks: Considering non-monetary benefits and perks as part of the negotiation.

b. Other Workplace Negotiations:

Promotions and Career Advancements: Preparing arguments based on performance and added value to the organization.

Workload and Responsibilities: Negotiating workload adjustments or changes in job roles to enhance job satisfaction.

3. Building Confidence to Negotiate Successfully:

a. Self-Assessment:

Identify Strengths: Recognizing personal strengths and skills that contribute to effective negotiation.

Address Weaknesses: Working on areas of improvement, such as assertiveness or emotional intelligence.

b. Practice and Role-Playing:

Mock Negotiations: Practicing negotiation scenarios with peers or mentors to build confidence.

Feedback and Reflection: Seeking feedback and reflecting on negotiation experiences to refine skills.

c. Mindset and Preparation:

Positive Mindset: Adopting a positive attitude towards negotiations and viewing them as opportunities for mutual gain.

Visualization: Visualizing successful negotiation outcomes to enhance confidence and motivation.

4. Overcoming Challenges in Negotiation:

a. Dealing with Resistance:

Handling Objections: Addressing concerns or objections raised by the other party calmly and respectfully.

Negotiating Deadlocks: Using problem-solving techniques to break deadlocks and keep negotiations moving forward.

b. Managing Emotions:

Emotional Intelligence: Recognizing and managing emotions effectively during negotiations.

Maintaining Professionalism: Staying composed and professional, even in challenging negotiation situations.

5. Conclusion:

Chapter 42 emphasizes the importance of developing negotiation skills as a critical component of professional success. By mastering key principles, preparing thoroughly for negotiations, and building confidence through practice and self-assessment, individuals can navigate various workplace negotiations effectively. The chapter would encourage continuous learning, adaptation to different negotiation contexts, and proactive engagement in negotiations to achieve favorable outcomes and career advancement.

Chapter 43: Staying Grounded - Stress Management Techniques

1. Recognizing and Understanding Workplace Stress:
a. Sources of Workplace Stress:
Job Demands: High workload, tight deadlines, or conflicting priorities.
Role Ambiguity: Unclear job responsibilities or expectations.
Interpersonal Conflicts: Tensions with colleagues or supervisors.
Organizational Factors: Changes in leadership, restructuring, or job insecurity.
b. Impact of Stress:
Physical Effects: Symptoms such as headaches, fatigue, or sleep disturbances.
Emotional Effects: Anxiety, irritability, or mood swings.
Cognitive Effects: Difficulty concentrating, memory problems, or decision-making challenges.
Behavioral Effects: Changes in eating habits, social withdrawal, or increased substance use.
2. Techniques for Reducing Stress and Increasing Resilience:
a. Stress Management Strategies:

Time Management: Prioritizing tasks, setting realistic goals, and using effective planning techniques.

Mindfulness and Meditation: Practicing mindfulness exercises, deep breathing, or meditation to reduce stress levels.

Physical Activity: Incorporating regular exercise or movement breaks to alleviate tension and boost mood.

Relaxation Techniques: Using techniques like progressive muscle relaxation or guided imagery to promote relaxation.

b. Cognitive Behavioral Techniques:

Cognitive Restructuring: Identifying and challenging negative thought patterns or irrational beliefs.

Problem-Solving Skills: Developing strategies to address and resolve work-related challenges effectively.

Assertiveness Training: Learning to assert one's needs and boundaries in a constructive manner.

3. Creating a Healthy Work Environment:

a. Organizational Support:

Workplace Policies: Implementing policies that promote work-life balance, flexibility, and employee well-being.

Employee Assistance Programs (EAP): Providing access to counseling services and resources for stress management.

Communication and Feedback: Encouraging open communication, feedback mechanisms, and employee involvement in decision-making processes.

b. Promoting a Positive Culture:

Leadership Role: Modeling stress management behaviors and promoting a supportive work culture.

Team Building: Fostering positive relationships among colleagues through team-building activities and recognition programs.

Workplace Wellness Initiatives: Offering wellness programs, workshops, or seminars on stress management and resilience.

4. Addressing Chronic Stress and Burnout:

a. Recognizing Warning Signs:

Burnout Symptoms: Exhaustion, cynicism, and reduced professional efficacy.

Seeking Help: Encouraging individuals to seek support from supervisors, HR, or mental health professionals.

b. Work-Life Integration:

Setting Boundaries: Establishing clear boundaries between work and personal life to prevent burnout.

Self-Care Practices: Prioritizing self-care activities such as hobbies, relaxation, and spending time with loved ones.

5. Evaluating and Adjusting Stress Management Strategies:

a. Continuous Assessment:

Monitoring Progress: Assessing the effectiveness of stress management techniques and making adjustments as needed.

Feedback Mechanisms: Soliciting feedback from employees to identify stressors and improve support systems.

6. Conclusion:

Chapter 43 underscores the importance of proactive stress management in creating a positive and productive work environment. By recognizing sources of stress, implementing effective coping strategies, and fostering organizational support and wellness initiatives, individuals and organizations can mitigate the impact of workplace stress, enhance resilience, and promote overall well-being. The chapter would emphasize collaboration between employees and employers in creating a culture that values mental health, communication, and work-life balance to sustain long-term professional success and satisfaction.

Chapter 44: The Entrepreneurial Spirit - Exploring Entrepreneurship

1. Considering Entrepreneurship as a Career Path:
a. Definition of Entrepreneurship:
Entrepreneurial Mindset: Exploring the mindset and characteristics of successful entrepreneurs.
Opportunities and Challenges: Discussing the opportunities and challenges of starting and running a business.
b. Motivations for Entrepreneurship:
Freedom and Independence: Seeking autonomy in decision-making and pursuing personal passions.
Innovation and Creativity: Opportunities to innovate and create new products, services, or solutions.
Financial Potential: Potential for financial rewards and wealth creation through successful ventures.
2. Essential Skills for Aspiring Entrepreneurs:
a. Leadership and Vision:

Visionary Thinking: Developing a clear vision and strategy for the business.

Decision-Making: Making informed decisions under uncertainty and ambiguity.

b. Adaptability and Resilience:

Adaptability: Being flexible and responsive to market changes and customer feedback.

Resilience: Handling setbacks, failures, and challenges with perseverance and determination.

c. Financial Literacy:

Budgeting and Financial Planning: Understanding cash flow management, budgeting, and financial projections.

Risk Management: Assessing and mitigating financial risks associated with entrepreneurship.

d. Communication and Networking:

Networking Skills: Building and nurturing relationships with stakeholders, investors, and customers.

Pitching and Selling: Effectively communicating the business idea and value proposition to potential partners and customers.

3. Balancing Risk and Reward in Entrepreneurship:

a. Risk Assessment:

Identifying Risks: Analyzing potential risks such as market competition, financial uncertainties, and regulatory challenges.

Risk Mitigation: Developing strategies to mitigate risks and uncertainties through contingency planning and diversification.

b. Reward Potential:

Financial Rewards: Discussing the potential for financial success and profitability in entrepreneurship.

Non-Financial Rewards: Recognizing the personal fulfillment and satisfaction of building and growing a successful venture.

c. Strategies for Managing Risk:

Lean Startup Methodology: Testing business ideas and prototypes quickly and cost-effectively to minimize initial investment.

Bootstrapping: Self-funding and resourceful management of financial resources to reduce dependence on external funding.

4. Entrepreneurship as a Continuous Learning Journey:

a. Lifelong Learning:

Continuous Improvement: Pursuing professional development and acquiring new skills to adapt to evolving market trends.

Market Research: Conducting ongoing market research and staying updated on industry developments.

b. Mentoring and Guidance:

Seeking Mentorship: Learning from experienced entrepreneurs and industry experts for guidance and advice.

Peer Support: Building a network of fellow entrepreneurs for knowledge sharing and support.

5. Conclusion:

Chapter 44 emphasizes the entrepreneurial journey as a dynamic and rewarding career path that requires a combination of skills, mindset, and strategic decision-making. By understanding the risks and rewards of entrepreneurship, aspiring entrepreneurs can prepare themselves effectively, leverage opportunities, and navigate challenges to build successful and sustainable ventures. The chapter would encourage aspiring entrepreneurs to embrace innovation, resilience, and continuous learning as key pillars of entrepreneurial success, contributing to economic growth, innovation, and societal impact.

Chapter 45: Standing Firm - Building Assertiveness in the Workplace

1. Understanding the Difference between Assertiveness and Aggression:
a. Definition of Assertiveness:
Assertive Communication: Clearly expressing thoughts, feelings, and needs in a direct and respectful manner.
Confidence: Assertiveness involves self-assurance without infringing on the rights of others.
b. Characteristics of Aggression:
Hostility: Aggressive behavior often involves hostility, intimidation, or disrespect towards others.
Conflict: Aggression may escalate conflict rather than seeking constructive resolution.

2. Techniques for Becoming More Assertive:
a. Assertive Communication Skills:
Clear and Direct Communication: Expressing thoughts and opinions in a straightforward manner.
Active Listening: Paying attention to others' viewpoints and responding appropriately.
b. Setting Boundaries:
Defining Limits: Clearly establishing personal boundaries and expectations.
Asserting Needs: Communicating personal needs and preferences without apology.
c. Assertive Body Language:
Confident Posture: Maintaining eye contact, standing or sitting upright, and using open gestures.
Voice Tone: Speaking in a firm but respectful tone, avoiding aggression or passivity.

3. Benefits of Assertiveness for Career Advancement:
a. Professional Respect and Recognition:
Leadership Qualities: Assertive individuals are often perceived as confident and capable leaders.
Effective Decision-Making: Assertiveness fosters the ability to make decisions and take initiative.
b. Conflict Resolution:
Effective Negotiation: Resolving conflicts and negotiating agreements calmly and constructively.
Team Collaboration: Building positive relationships and promoting teamwork through assertive communication.
c. Career Growth and Opportunities:
Opportunity Seizing: Assertive individuals are more likely to pursue and seize career opportunities.
Self-Advocacy: Advocating for career advancement, promotions, or salary increases.

4. Overcoming Challenges to Assertiveness:
a. Fear of Rejection or Conflict:
Building Confidence: Developing self-confidence and resilience to manage fear of rejection.

Conflict Management Skills: Learning strategies to address and resolve conflicts assertively.

b. Cultural and Organizational Factors:

Respecting Diversity: Adapting assertiveness techniques to cultural norms and organizational culture.

Seeking Support: Seeking guidance from mentors or coaches to navigate assertiveness challenges.

5. Practicing Assertiveness in Everyday Situations:

a. Role-Playing and Practice:

Simulated Scenarios: Engaging in role-playing exercises to practice assertive communication.

Feedback and Reflection: Seeking feedback and reflecting on assertiveness skills to improve over time.

6. Conclusion:

Chapter 45 highlights assertiveness as a valuable skill for professional success, emphasizing its role in effective communication, conflict resolution, and career advancement. By mastering assertiveness techniques, individuals can cultivate a positive work environment, build constructive relationships, and assert their needs and ambitions confidently. The chapter would encourage continuous development of assertiveness skills as a cornerstone of professional growth, contributing to personal empowerment and organizational effectiveness in diverse workplace settings.

Chapter 46: The Growth Mindset - Strategies for Career Growth

1. Understanding the Growth Mindset:
a. Definition and Characteristics:
Belief in Growth: Embracing the belief that abilities and intelligence can be developed through effort and learning.
Resilience: Viewing challenges as opportunities for learning and growth rather than setbacks.
b. Contrasting with Fixed Mindset:
Fixed vs. Growth Mindset: Highlighting the differences in attitudes towards challenges, feedback, and effort.
Impact on Behavior: How mindset influences motivation, resilience, and willingness to take on new challenges.
2. Strategies for Adopting a Growth Mindset:
a. Embracing Challenges:
Seeking Stretch Assignments: Volunteering for projects that push one's skills and abilities.

Learning from Failure: Viewing setbacks as learning opportunities and identifying lessons for improvement.

b. Developing Persistence:

Perseverance: Maintaining effort and determination in the face of obstacles or setbacks.

Long-term Goals: Setting ambitious yet achievable goals for continuous improvement.

c. Cultivating Curiosity and Learning:

Continuous Learning: Actively seeking out opportunities for professional development, such as courses, workshops, or certifications.

Feedback Orientation: Welcoming feedback as a tool for growth and improvement.

3. Seeking Out Opportunities for Advancement:

a. Career Planning and Goal Setting:

Setting Clear Objectives: Establishing short-term and long-term career goals aligned with personal values and aspirations.

Networking and Mentorship: Building relationships with mentors, sponsors, and peers to explore career opportunities and receive guidance.

b. Taking Initiative:

Proactive Approach: Identifying gaps or opportunities within the organization and proposing solutions or new initiatives.

Professional Development: Pursuing opportunities for skill development and acquiring new competencies relevant to career goals.

4. Overcoming Obstacles to Career Growth:

a. Identifying and Addressing Challenges:

Self-Assessment: Assessing strengths, weaknesses, and areas for improvement to overcome obstacles.

Resilience Building: Developing coping strategies to manage setbacks and challenges effectively.

b. Managing Change:

Adaptability: Being open to change and embracing new roles or responsibilities as opportunities for growth.

Networking and Support: Leveraging support networks and seeking advice from mentors or colleagues during challenging times.

5. Cultivating a Growth-Oriented Culture:

a. Leadership and Organizational Support:

Encouraging Innovation: Fostering a culture that values creativity, experimentation, and continuous improvement.

Recognition and Rewards: Acknowledging and celebrating achievements and efforts towards personal and organizational growth.

6. Conclusion:

Chapter 46 emphasizes the importance of adopting a growth mindset as a catalyst for career growth and development. By embracing challenges, persisting through setbacks, and actively seeking opportunities for advancement, individuals can cultivate resilience, adaptability, and a commitment to lifelong learning. The chapter would encourage readers to reflect on their mindset, set ambitious goals, and leverage strategies and resources to navigate obstacles and achieve professional success in dynamic and competitive work environments.

Chapter 47: Finding Fulfillment - Enhancing Job Satisfaction

1. Factors Contributing to Job Satisfaction:
a. Work Environment:
Organizational Culture: Assessing how values, norms, and practices align with personal values.
Relationships: Building positive relationships with colleagues, supervisors, and team members.
Work-Life Balance: Balancing work demands with personal and family responsibilities.
b. Job Characteristics:
Role Clarity: Understanding job responsibilities and expectations.
Autonomy and Control: Having a degree of independence in decision-making and task management.
Skill Utilization: Using skills and competencies effectively in daily tasks.
c. Compensation and Benefits:
Fair Compensation: Feeling adequately compensated for skills, experience, and contributions.

Benefits Package: Evaluating benefits such as healthcare, retirement plans, and professional development opportunities.

d. Personal Growth and Development:

Career Advancement: Opportunities for promotion, skill development, and career progression.

Learning Opportunities: Access to training, workshops, and certifications to enhance skills.

2. Making Adjustments to Increase Job Satisfaction:

a. Assessing Current Satisfaction Levels:

Self-Reflection: Reflecting on current job satisfaction levels and identifying areas for improvement.

Feedback: Seeking feedback from colleagues, supervisors, or mentors on performance and satisfaction.

b. Addressing Dissatisfaction:

Problem Solving: Identifying specific factors causing dissatisfaction and developing action plans to address them.

Communicating Needs: Articulating needs and concerns constructively with supervisors or HR.

c. Seeking Meaningful Tasks:

Task Variety: Seeking opportunities for diverse tasks that align with skills and interests.

Project Ownership: Taking ownership of projects or initiatives that contribute to personal growth and organizational goals.

3. Pursuing Meaningful Work and Purpose:

a. Aligning Values and Purpose:

Personal Values: Evaluating how work aligns with personal values and beliefs.

Impact and Contribution: Finding meaning in work that contributes positively to society or the organization.

b. Finding Passion and Engagement:

Passion Projects: Pursuing projects or initiatives that spark passion and enthusiasm.

Engagement: Engaging fully in tasks and responsibilities that resonate with personal interests and career goals.

4. Overcoming Challenges to Job Satisfaction:

a. Managing Stress and Burnout:
Stress Management: Implementing stress reduction techniques such as mindfulness, exercise, or time management.
Work-Life Integration: Establishing boundaries and prioritizing self-care to prevent burnout.
b. Addressing Career Plateaus:
Skill Development: Pursuing professional development opportunities to acquire new skills and advance career prospects.
Seeking New Challenges: Exploring opportunities for growth within the current organization or considering new career paths.

5. Creating a Plan for Enhanced Job Satisfaction:
a. Setting Goals:
SMART Goals: Setting specific, measurable, achievable, relevant, and time-bound goals for increasing satisfaction.
Action Steps: Developing a plan with actionable steps to achieve desired improvements.
b. Monitoring Progress:
Regular Evaluation: Assessing progress towards enhancing satisfaction and adjusting strategies as needed.
Feedback Loop: Seeking feedback from supervisors, peers, or mentors to gauge improvements and areas for further development.

6. Conclusion:
Chapter 47 emphasizes the importance of proactive measures to enhance job satisfaction and fulfillment in one's career. By identifying key factors influencing satisfaction, making targeted adjustments, and aligning work with personal values and purpose, individuals can cultivate a sense of fulfillment, motivation, and commitment in their professional lives. The chapter would encourage continuous reflection, adaptation, and pursuit of meaningful work to achieve long-term career satisfaction and personal well-being.

Conclusion: Your Path Forward

As you reflect on the journey through these chapters, several key themes and takeaways have emerged, guiding your path forward towards achieving long-term career success and personal fulfillment.

Recap of Key Themes and Takeaways
Throughout this exploration, you've encountered essential principles and strategies across various aspects of professional and personal growth:

Self-Development and Skills: Embracing continuous learning and skill enhancement as foundational to adapting and thriving in dynamic environments.

Communication and Relationships: Recognizing the significance of effective communication, building relationships, and navigating workplace dynamics with empathy and professionalism.

Leadership and Influence: Cultivating leadership qualities, whether leading teams or influencing others positively, to drive collective success.

Resilience and Well-being: Prioritizing resilience, managing stress, and fostering work-life balance to sustain long-term health and performance.

Goal Setting and Achievement: Setting clear goals, both short-term and long-term, and employing strategies to maintain focus and motivation towards their attainment.

Encouragement for Ongoing Professional and Personal Growth
As you continue your journey, here are some words of encouragement:

Embrace Change: Stay agile and adaptable in navigating the evolving landscape of your career. View challenges as opportunities for growth and learning.

Seek Mentorship: Engage with mentors and peers who can offer guidance, support, and diverse perspectives to broaden your horizons.

Invest in Relationships: Foster meaningful connections within your professional network. Collaborate, mentor, and learn from others to enrich your career journey.

Celebrate Milestones: Acknowledge your achievements and milestones along the way. Celebrate successes, big and small, to stay motivated and inspired.

Prioritize Well-being: Remember that sustainable success is rooted in well-being. Take time for self-care, hobbies, and activities that rejuvenate your mind and body.

Final Thoughts on Achieving Long-term Career Success

As you envision your future and strive for long-term career success:

Define Your Vision: Clarify your vision of success and what it means to you personally and professionally.

Stay Committed to Growth: Commit to lifelong learning and growth, embracing opportunities to develop new skills and expand your knowledge base.

Adapt and Innovate: Embrace innovation and creativity in your approach to challenges and opportunities, positioning yourself as a proactive agent of change.

Contribute Meaningfully: Seek roles and projects that align with your values and contribute positively to your organization and community.

Stay Positive and Resilient: Maintain a positive mindset, resilience in the face of setbacks, and optimism about your ability to create impact and achieve your goals.

Your path forward is as unique as you are, shaped by your experiences, aspirations, and the choices you make along the way. With dedication, perseverance, and a commitment to continuous improvement, you are well-equipped to navigate the complexities of the professional world and forge a fulfilling career journey.

Here's to your ongoing success and fulfillment in all your endeavors. Remember, the journey continues, and each step forward brings new opportunities for growth and achievement.

Appendix: Resources and Tools

In your pursuit of professional growth and career success, leveraging resources and tools can significantly enhance your journey. Here are some recommended resources to support various aspects of your development:

Skill Development and Learning Platforms:

LinkedIn Learning: Offers courses on a wide range of topics from leadership and communication to technical skills.
Coursera: Provides online courses from universities and organizations worldwide, covering diverse fields.
Udemy: Features a vast collection of courses taught by experts in business, technology, and creative fields.
Books for Professional Development:

"Drive: The Surprising Truth About What Motivates Us" by Daniel H. Pink: Explores the science of motivation and what drives individuals to succeed.
"Emotional Intelligence 2.0" by Travis Bradberry and Jean Greaves: Guides readers on developing emotional intelligence for effective leadership and interpersonal relationships.

"Atomic Habits: An Easy & Proven Way to Build Good Habits & Break Bad Ones" by James Clear: Provides strategies for building productive habits and achieving personal goals.

Networking and Career Advancement:

Professional Associations: Join industry-specific associations to network with peers, attend events, and access career resources.

LinkedIn: Utilize LinkedIn for networking, job searches, industry insights, and professional branding.

Meetup: Attend local or virtual meetups to connect with professionals sharing similar interests or career paths.

Career Planning and Assessment Tools:

StrengthsFinder: Helps identify and leverage your top strengths for career development.

Myers-Briggs Type Indicator (MBTI): Provides insights into personality preferences and potential career paths.

Career One Stop: Offers tools for career exploration, resume building, and job searches.

Well-being and Stress Management:

Calm or Headspace: Apps for guided meditation, relaxation techniques, and stress reduction.

Physical Activity Apps: Such as Strava or Nike Training Club for fitness routines and maintaining physical well-being.

Professional Development Workshops and Webinars:

Toastmasters International: Provides public speaking and leadership development opportunities through local clubs.

Local Chambers of Commerce: Often host workshops on business skills, networking, and entrepreneurship.

Financial Management and Planning:

Personal Finance Books: Such as "Rich Dad Poor Dad" by Robert T. Kiyosaki or "The Total Money Makeover" by Dave Ramsey for financial education and planning.

Financial Planning Tools: Mint or YNAB for budgeting, expense tracking, and financial goal setting.

Online Tools for Productivity and Organization:

Evernote: For note-taking, organization, and task management.

Trello: Visual project management tool for planning and tracking tasks.

Google Workspace (formerly G Suite): Offers tools like Google Docs, Sheets, and Drive for collaboration and productivity.

Conclusion

These resources and tools are designed to complement your journey towards professional growth, personal development, and career satisfaction. Continuously explore, learn, and adapt these resources to align with your goals and aspirations. Remember, your commitment to ongoing learning and improvement will pave the way for long-term success in your career and beyond.

Wishing you all the best in your endeavors and may you find fulfillment and achievement in every step of your professional journey.

Skill Development and Learning Platforms:

LinkedIn Learning - Offers courses on business, technology, and creative skills.

Coursera - Provides online courses from universities and organizations worldwide.

Udemy - Features a wide range of courses taught by experts in various fields.

Networking and Career Advancement:
LinkedIn - A professional networking platform for connecting with peers, finding jobs, and industry insights.

Meetup - Facilitates connecting with local or virtual groups based on shared interests or professional goals.

Books for Professional Development:
Drive: The Surprising Truth About What Motivates Us by Daniel H. Pink - Explores motivation and success.

Emotional Intelligence 2.0 by Travis Bradberry and Jean Greaves - Focuses on emotional intelligence for leadership.

Atomic Habits: An Easy & Proven Way to Build Good Habits & Break Bad Ones by James Clear - Offers strategies for habit formation and personal growth.

Well-being and Stress Management Apps:
Calm - Provides guided meditation, relaxation, and sleep resources.

Headspace - Offers meditation and mindfulness exercises for stress reduction.

Professional Development Workshops and Webinars:
Toastmasters International - Helps improve public speaking and leadership skills through local clubs.
Financial Management and Planning:
Mint - Offers tools for budgeting, expense tracking, and financial goal setting.

You Need A Budget (YNAB) - Helps users manage finances through budgeting and financial planning.

Productivity and Organization Tools:
Evernote - A note-taking and organization app for capturing ideas and managing tasks.

Trello - Visual project management tool for organizing tasks and projects.

Google Workspace - Includes Google Docs, Sheets, Drive, and other productivity tools for collaboration.

Additional Tools for Career Development:

StrengthsFinder - Identifies individual strengths and talents for career development.

CareerOneStop - Provides tools for career exploration, resume building, and job searches.

These resources and tools are designed to support your professional growth, career advancement, and personal well-being. Explore them according to your needs and interests, and leverage them to achieve your career goals effectively.

Comprehensive Index

Active Listening and Persuasive Communication
Leadership Skills
Key Qualities of Effective Leaders
Leadership Styles and When to Use Them
Networking for Success
Importance of Professional Networking
Building and Maintaining a Strong Network
Leveraging Networking Opportunities for Career Growth
Time Management Techniques
Strategies for Effective Time Management
Prioritizing Tasks and Avoiding Procrastination
Work-Life Balance
Importance for Long-term Success
Strategies for Managing Work and Personal Life
Setting Boundaries and Making Time for Self-care
Goal Setting for Professional Growth
Techniques for Setting and Achieving Goals
Creating Short-term and Long-term Career Plans
Evaluating and Adjusting Goals as Needed
Understanding Workplace Culture

Importance for Career Satisfaction
Navigating and Adapting to Different Cultures
Contributing Positively to Workplace Culture
Negotiation Skills
Principles of Effective Negotiation
Preparing for Salary and Workplace Negotiations
Building Confidence for Successful Negotiation
Stress Management Techniques
Recognizing and Managing Workplace Stress
Reducing Stress and Increasing Resilience
Creating a Healthy Work Environment
Entrepreneurship
Considering Entrepreneurship as a Career Path
Essential Skills for Entrepreneurs
Balancing Risk and Reward in Entrepreneurship
Career Transitions
Identifying When It's Time for a Change
Planning and Executing a Career Transition
Overcoming Challenges During a Career Shift
Job Satisfaction and Fulfillment
Factors Contributing to Job Satisfaction
Making Adjustments to Increase Satisfaction
Pursuing Meaningful Work and Purpose
Assertiveness in the Workplace
Difference Between Assertiveness and Aggression
Techniques for Building Assertiveness
Benefits for Career Advancement
Growth Mindset for Career Growth
Adopting a Growth Mindset for Improvement
Seeking Opportunities for Advancement
Overcoming Obstacles to Growth
Professional Development and Personal Growth
Resources and Tools for Skill Development
Networking Platforms and Career Advancement
Books and Apps for Well-being and Stress Management
Productivity and Organization Tools

Tools for Time Management and Efficiency
Financial Management and Planning Resources
Tools for Personal and Professional Organization
How to Use This Index
This index serves as a quick reference guide to revisit specific topics and concepts covered throughout your journey of professional and personal growth. Use it to navigate chapters, find detailed information on particular subjects, and reinforce learning across various dimensions of career development and well-being. Whether seeking strategies for effective communication, leadership insights, or tools for managing stress, this index directs you to relevant sections for deeper exploration and application in your professional life.

www.ingramcontent.com/pod-product-compliance
Lightning Source LLC
Chambersburg PA
CBHW071452220526
45472CB00003B/766